KT-169-610

Personal Life
New directions in sociological thinking

CAROL SMART

polity

Copyright © Carol Smart 2007

The right of Carol Smart to be identified as Author of this Work has been asserted in accordance with the UK Copyright, Designs and Patents Act 1988.

First published in 2007 by Polity Press
Reprinted 2008

Polity Press
65 Bridge Street
Cambridge CB2 1UR, UK

Polity Press
350 Main Street
Malden, MA 02148, USA

All rights reserved. Except for the quotation of short passages for the purpose of criticism and review, no part of this publication may be reproduced, stored in a retrieval system, or transmitted, in any form or by any means, electronic, mechanical, photocopying, recording or otherwise, without the prior permission of the publisher.

ISBN-13: 978-07456-3916-1
ISBN-13: 978-07456-3917-8 (pb)

A catalogue record for this book is available from the British Library.

Typeset in 11 on 13pt Bembo
by Servis Filmsetting Ltd, Manchester
Printed and bound in Great Britain by MPG Books Ltd, Bodmin, Cornwall

The publisher has used its best endeavours to ensure that the URLs for external websites referred to in this book are correct and active at the time of going to press. However, the publisher has no responsibility for the websites and can make no guarantee that a site will remain live or that the content is or will remain appropriate.

Every effort has been made to trace all copyright holders, but if any have been inadvertently overlooked the publisher will be pleased to include any necessary credits in any subsequent reprint or edition.

For further information on Polity, visit our website: www.polity.co.uk

Contents

List of Illustrations

Acknowledgements

I am indebted to my colleagues in the Morgan Centre for the Study of Relationships and Personal Life at the University of Manchester for providing the immensely supportive and intellectually exciting context within which I was able to write this book. In particular I wish to thank Jennifer Mason, Brian Heaphy, Vanessa May, Wendy Bottero and Dale Southerton who have all contributed substantially to my understanding of personal life. Other forms of intellectual support have come from colleagues whose work has been inspirational, including David Morgan, Janet Finch and John Gillis. Those with whom I have worked on previous research projects must also be acknowledged for their intellectual generosity and hard graft. These include Bren Neale, Amanda Wade, Beccy Shipman and Jennifer Flowerdew. And, in addition, I want to give thanks to the ESRC, the Nuffield Foundation and the Joseph Rowntree Foundation, all of whom have funded the various projects drawn upon in this book, and to the University of Manchester for allowing me time to write. Finally my most personal thanks go to John Adams.

Introduction

Some years ago I became the keeper of my family's photographs. I 'inherited' them from my mother, whose main reason for keeping them seemed solely that she hated throwing *anything* away. They were not cherished but thrown together in no order at all in a large carrier bag. My mother was not the sort to spend time putting photos in albums with helpful captions and dates. Having inherited them I then found I could not throw them away either and so they lived for about two decades in the same plastic bag until I was left another batch from a maternal aunt – this time kept with slightly more reverence in an old sewing box. I was prompted to start sorting them, a task as yet unfinished. In the processes I found myself going through a journey of the imagination, of memory, of emotion and of history. I found photographs of relatives I had never met and of whom I had only the dimmest knowledge. Take the couple overleaf whom I know to be my paternal grandparents. They died when my father was twelve years old and all I know about them is that my grandfather was a butcher with a stall on Harrow Road in West London sometime after the First World War.

I found myself trying to imagine their lives and to read into the photograph whether they were happy or not, whether their lives were very hard or reasonably comfortable, whether they were

Plate 1.1   My paternal grandparents

respected members of their community or not. On the third point
I have to confess that the photograph conveys an ambivalent relationship with respectability. I suppose one can say that at least they
are standing outside the (more respectable) 'Saloon Bar' of the
public house rather than the (rougher) 'Public Bar'. My grandfather is wearing a suit and my grandmother sports a hat – it must
be a Sunday afternoon. But he looks distinctly shifty, possibly even
a bit menacing, perhaps because of his fedora (hat), the creases in
the suit and the manner of cupping his cigarette to his lips. Her coat
has seen better days, while her hat and shabby fox stole suggest
a certain working-class flamboyance not exactly associated with
(refined) feminine respectability. Moreover, they are pictured
together outside a pub (not a church or more salubrious venue) and
my grandfather's slightly louche pose against the door frame suggests that he was a regular, definitely familiar with the place.

I love this photograph. Whenever I look at it I wish I could step
into it and back in time to ask them questions or merely to observe
them. I do not, of course, feel like this about any old photograph, so
this is not a generalized desire. The only reason I want to step back
to be near these people is because I believe them to be related to me
and this sense of connectedness across the generations means I want
to know more about them, their daily lives, their feelings, their
views, their aspirations and so on. These people are so (apparently)

different from me and yet also connected. I can envisage this as a link that comes through my father to me in the form of small physical resemblances, or in terms of shared genes, knowing that some (almost) invisible, intangible part of them is somewhere alive in me. Alternatively my connection with them can be construed through place, because they lived and died in the same area of London in which I was brought up. Or I can understand the connection in terms of my own upbringing, since they raised my father (at least until their early deaths) and I therefore enjoyed (or endured) the kind of parenting that their practices had induced in my own father.

Although I feel all these things and these emotions are real to me, I also know that these connections and impressions are largely works of personal/cultural fiction. What I have expressed here in personal terms, I know to be a cultural phenomenon and that these (and similar) experiences are being felt at the same time by many people who have become interested in genealogy and family history in late modern societies. Sociologically speaking, I am part of a minor social movement; both interest in and sentimental feelings about the past of one's family is heavily encouraged by the family heritage industry as well as by new technologies such as the world wide web and online census and historical data banks. At a more subtle level I also understand that memories, for example of my own childhood and those 'implanted' by my parents of things that occurred before I was born, are part of a sense of self. Dealing with family photos is not simply a hobby, but part of an active and culturally specific production of the self. It is therefore possible not only to know that feelings are constructed and plastic, but to work with them and find meaning in them. It is this relationship between knowing (or thinking we know) how cultural and social practices are brought into being and sustained, and being part of the culture and the historical moment, that provided one of the main intellectual motivations for me to write this book. In other words I wanted to write sociologically about relationships and connectedness while remaining grounded in, and even working with, the kinds of real feelings generated by relating to others. I wanted to move out of the flat world of most sociological accounts of relationships and families to incorporate the kinds of emotional and relational dimensions that are meaningful in everyday life. I felt it was no longer appropriate to reflect upon 'other' people as if being a sociologist entitled one to be apart from these cultural shifts, emotional tides and personal feelings. It is true that the sociologist should not assume that what s/he feels and experiences is common to all, but I am suggesting a more reflexive engagement than this would imply. I also wanted to capture the importance of the past and of imagination to the living of family life and relationships. Although, following David Morgan (1996), I acknowledge that family is what families do, I also think we need to explore those families and relationships which exist in our imaginings and memories, since these are just as real. In the past this realm of imagination was construed sociologically as the work of dominant ideologies; attachment to ideals of family and kin connectedness were understood in terms of false-consciousness or class interest. This prompted a focus on the material and on social action rather than mentalities. Understanding the realms of yearning, desires and inner emotions in different ways has opened up a whole new domain for thoughtful exploration.

My relationship with this book is therefore distinct from those I have had with previous volumes that I have authored or co-authored. My motivation to incorporate dimensions that I think have been overlooked or understated comes, as I suggest above, partly from my own reflexive engagement with kith and kin. This does not mean that I have written only about what matters to me. On the contrary I have tried to stretch the reach of the sociology of family life beyond established boundaries. So this is not a book about my feelings or experiences. It is motivated by of my experience that a lot of sociology, and most particularly recent theories of individualization, do not capture sufficiently the richness of the life world. An equally important reason for writing slightly differently this time has come from experiences arising from engagement in a significant number of qualitative research projects over the last ten years. I came to feel that the lives of ordinary people were being flattened out and that I was in part complicit in this. Although in these various projects we sought to do justice to the lives we described and analysed, I am not sure that I then had sufficient analytical tools available. Too much was left on the cutting-room floor, so to speak. And so in this book I have revisited a number of these projects, re-examining some of the interviews we carried out in search of further ideas and dimensions. I do this with a 'light touch', by which I mean that I do not report fully on these projects as that would deflect from my main purpose. In returning to these stories, I aim to allow expression to some of the less tangible elements of the relational lives of those to whom we spoke. I have felt it necessary to change the names and some of the details in these accounts for the sake of anonymity, but I have tried not to alter the cultural meanings and signifiers. Through this I strive to do something new in providing a conceptual framework for the ways in which we can develop different analytical approaches for understanding and capturing personal life sociologically. I map out overlapping core concepts with which it should be possible to frame more subtle research questions in order that feelings, emotions, memories, biographies and connections do not remain afterthoughts but can be built into original research questions.

Finally I have a small confession to make. As with many long writing projects, especially those of an exploratory nature, sometimes the scope, reach and meaning of the text become apparent to the author only towards the end. This has been my experience with this book. Although I had certain clear goals (namely the critique of theories of individualization, the construction of alternative conceptual frameworks, the introduction of different fields of enquiry and so on), for me the act of writing is a form of engagement in which ideas change even as they appear on the page. What is more these ideas do not appear on the page without struggle: they slip about and move out of sight; they refuse to take shape and then, when they do, the shape often turns out to be quite wrong. So the idea of defining a conceptual field known as personal life was not my original intention; this emerged partway through the writing. This inevitably means that the project is unfinished. Having completed the groundwork, I now feel there is so much more work to do. I hope to continue with this theme in the near future; perhaps this book will be followed by *Personal Life*, volume 2. But in the meantime I have yet more photographs to sort out.

1

A Sociology of Personal Life

In this chapter I formulate an argument for developing a sociology of personal life which can embrace what has traditionally been known as the sociology of the family and the sociology of kinship but also more recent fields such as friendship, same-sex intimacies, acquaintanceship, relationships across households, and cross-cultural relationships. I suggest that this field is not simply a convenient 'holdall' for old and new empirical areas of study, but also a way of bringing together conceptual and theoretical developments which now seem too uncomfortable when squeezed into the existing terminologies of families or partnering or parenting. Sociology has periodically tried to rid itself of the conceptual and political straitjacket that the concept of 'the family' imposes, either by talking instead of 'households', or by introducing 'families of choice', by preferring the term 'kinship', or by conceptualizing relationships more in terms of practices than institutions or structures. These shifts in terminology and the conceptualizations that accompany them have loosened the constraints and have allowed the old terminology of family to become less rigidly identified with the idealized white, nuclear heterosexual families of Western cultures in the 1950s. However, it seems clear that in spite of these advances, the terminology of family (whether plural or not, chosen or not), and the other specifications of kinship or household, still prioritize biological connectedness and/or physical place. The term 'family' generally conjures up an image of degrees of biological relatedness combined with degrees of co-residence. Yet we know that people relate meaningfully and significantly to one another across distances, in different places and also when there is no pre-given genetic or even legal bond. These relationships may be described as 'networks' because this term is not evocative of a particular place and it also allows for fluidity in membership. But that term robs the concept of relationships of much of its emotional content and certainly does not invoke the special importance of connectedness, biography and memory in how people relate to one another. So it seems to me important to start to conceptualize a different field of vision in which families appear, but where 'the family' is not automatically the centrepiece against which other forms of relationship must be measured, or in whose long shadow all research is carried out. In sketching out this field of vision I neither fill in every contour, nor make every conceivable connection. Rather I aim to illuminate spheres and issues which make up the most significant elements of a newly conceived field of personal life. As I say in my introduction, this is not a finished project but a starting point. However, before arriving at my discussion of the ideas that constitute this field, I feel it is necessary to sketch the intellectual terrain covered thus far and, in particular, to explore the theoretical stresses and strains that have been part of long-term academic (and political) discussions of family life, and most especially since Anthony Giddens published his *Transformation of Intimacy* in 1992 and Ulrich Beck and Elisabeth Beck-Gernsheim their *Normal Chaos of Love* in 1995.

Residues, traces and heritage: the sociological battle over the family

'Family research is only gradually waking up from its drowsy fixation on the nucleus of the family' (Beck and Beck-Gernsheim, 1995: 147). This polemical remark is somewhat inaccurate but for our purposes here it captures the issues which have formed a long-standing tension in the area of the sociology of family life; namely the tension between broad, generalized theoretical statements and small-scale, detailed empirical research. The battle between these approaches, which has reintensified since the mid-1990s, has taken a number of forms, occasionally almost finding a resolution and then breaking out into a form of academic warfare again. At the risk of oversimplifying the picture, it might be possible to say that broad theories of family life have been developed in relation to the trends in mainstream sociological theorizing, hence there have been functionalist theories (Parsons and Bales, 1955), Marxist theories (from Engels to some feminist work), feminist theories, and risk and individualization theories (Beck and Beck-Gernsheim, 1995). These approaches have developed as explanations of social change and social relationships rather than specifically in relation to family life, but have then been applied to explanations of the kinds of family change often 'revealed' in large-scale surveys and social statistics. As Brannen and Nilsen (2005) argue, these are not grounded theories because, although they may use some empirical research to supplement or support the core arguments, the driving intellectual force is deductive rather than inductive. On the other hand, empirical work on family life, especially the qualitative variety, has usually been small-scale, local, interpretive and averse to generalizations. Because such work has focused on particular groups of families in, for instance, the East End of London (Young and Willmott, 1987, orig. 1957), or Swansea (Rosser and Harris, 1983), or has selected special or minority groups such as Pakistani families (Shaw, 2000), same-sex couples (Weeks et al., 2001) or step-families (Ribbens McCarthy et al., 2003) it has rarely had an impact on sociological Thought (with a capital T). Taken together such studies have undoubtedly influenced sociological thinking and also methodology, but individually none of these appears to have set the sociological agenda or to have become the focus of intense debate.[1] Instead it is possible to see a kind of pattern developing since the 1950s in which there have been phases of grand theorizing in which understandings of family life are linked to wider social forces (industrialization, capitalism, post-war social order/functionalism, patriarchy and latterly globalization). Then, in the wake of these theories, empirical research sets about testing whether these explanations apply in specific circumstances or to particular groups. None of these studies can ever hope to 'prove' or 'disprove' the grand explanation, but they can either bolster or chip away at their credibility. In the main their efforts go unnoticed by the grander theoreticians. This is because general theories (and their authors) do not claim to explain 'detail'. So to complain that they misrepresent specific families, or that they oversimplify family life and relationships, is really only to state the obvious. Yet such theorizations do have to be challenged because they are not simply free-floating ideas, they have an influence on the kinds of sociological understanding which come to predominate and on the wider political and policy processes which take such depictions and explanations as truths around which policy decisions should be framed (Brannen and Nilsen, 2005; Smart, 2005b; Lewis, 2001). It is also possible to argue that certain sociological theories enter into everyday understandings of family life and family change such that they start to frame the context in which people in general experience their families − or at least how they perceive *other* people's families. As Brannen and Nilsen argue:

> When theoretical concepts are not grounded in local contexts they more easily lend themselves to rhetorical purposes and can take on an ideological aspect. [. . .] When such theories chime with dominant political discourse, they feed back into that society and gain even greater ideological and rhetorical power. (2005: 426)

Of course not all sociological theories and concepts necessarily become popular and Brannen and Nilsen suggest that for this to happen there needs to be a fit between the emergent concepts and a dominant political philosophy at a given time. The focus of their criticism is individualization theory's emphasis on the individual and on choice, which they see as chiming with neo-liberal ideologies of Western governments such as New Labour in the UK. However, before looking more closely at arguments over individualization, I endeavour to trace a longer history to the debate between broad theoretical work and smaller-scale empirical work in the area of family life. I consider early ideas and concepts and the tensions that arose as they became persuasive or dominant, as well as the ways in which concepts and ideas came to influence empirical work and also how empirical studies themselves – through the development of grounded theories – came to influence sociological thinking.

The great debates

Perhaps the most significant of these debates around family life have been those between (1) ideas of the demise of the extended family and the rise of the 'modern' nuclear family; (2) the decline of marriage as an economic contract and the rise of companionate relationships between spouses; (3) the changing status of childhood and the growth of child-centredness; (4) and latterly the decline of the nuclear family and the rise of fluid family practices.

The first of these, based in social history as much as sociology,[2] concerned the argument between two groups: those who felt that industrialization had changed the family, turning it from an economic unit of production with many children, strong kinship ties and embracing several generations into the small nuclear family of two parents and two children, cut off from kin and operating more as a unit of consumption; and those who point both to the continuation of extended kin networks in certain regions and in certain minority groups and to the lack of co-resident kinship groups before industrialization (Laslett, 2005, orig. 1965;[3] Macfarlane, 1979). Both sides of this debate have deployed empirical evidence, so it is not entirely accurate to depict the conflict simply in terms of grand theorizing versus empirical research, but nonetheless the former did generalize from certain trends and ultimately did see one type of family as being inevitable under conditions of industrialization and capitalism. The most tenacious in this approach were Talcott Parsons and Robert Bales (1955) who, through the framework of structural functionalism, explained changes to 'the family' in terms of the needs of modern capitalist societies. Thus they argued that the economic order came to require small families, with a high investment in fewer children, a clear division of labour between husbands and wives giving rise to efficiency in the labour market, and with the family as a unit of consumption rather than production which in turn suited the capitalist economy. Parsons and Bales saw the decline of the influence of the extended family as a 'good thing' because it allowed for the rise of meritocracy in place of nepotism; in their schema the small, nuclear family was morally superior as well as more efficient than the *traditional* extended family. Some fifty years or so later the 'new' nuclear family in Parsons and Bales of course became – in contemporary collective imaginings – the *traditional* family. Thus when critics of contemporary family forms warn of dire consequences stemming from the demise of the traditional family, they now often mean the nuclear married family; when Parsons and Bales were referring to the traditional family, however, they meant the pre-industrial extended family. Thus the concept of the 'traditional family' moves and reconfigures itself depending upon which discourse is being deployed at a given time. And, as I argue below, this blurred notion of the traditional family has cropped up again in later theories of individualization.

The second debate, about the rise of the companionate marriage, is also one that moves across decades and seems to have no very precise historical location. Thus Edward Shorter (1976) sees a long history to the development away from marriage as an alliance of families and domestic economies towards marriage as a form of partnership and companionship. As Leonore Davidoff et al. suggest: 'The popular perception is that the first to embrace the ideals of companionate marriage, separate spheres, innocent childhood and small families were the middle classes as they emerged from industrialization' (1999: 18). Yet later they argue:

> The growing belief in equality between partners, with husband and wife playing different but complementary roles, was an important element in the development of the 'companionate marriage' [. . .]. Promoted in the 1920s, as an argument for legalized birth control and divorce by mutual consent for childless couples, and reinforced even more strongly in the 1950s, this model was based upon the ideas of an exclusive emotionally and sexually intimate relationship between a man and a woman, satisfying to both partners. (1999: 190)

Companionate marriage (always a classed concept) therefore seems to have its genesis in the early nineteenth century, but with flashes of intensity in the 1920s and 1950s (Finch and Summerfield, 1991). A revival of a very similar idea comes with Giddens (1992) and his concept of confluent love and the pure relationship. The idea that this is something both new and caused by recent social changes and the growth of individualization is also adopted by Beck: 'The need for a shared inner life, as expressed in the ideal of marriage and bonding, is not a primeval need. It *grows* with the losses that individualisation brings as the obverse of its opportunities' (1992: 105; emphasis in original). So although social historians of the family have been dating the rise of the companionate marriage from at least the period of industrialization in England,[4] it recurs as something fresh and rather new at regular intervals throughout the twentieth century. Of course it is also possible to see this as a trend or as something that is simply intensifying and/or expanding over time, yet it is hard to avoid the inference that it is being regularly rediscovered with new waves of theoretical enthusiasm or new empirical research.

The third debate, about the changing status of children in families and the growth (or apparent growth) of child-centredness, follows similar lines of argument. Thus Linda Pollock (1983) takes issue with Philippe Ariès (1962, French orig. 1960) and his thesis that childhood as a distinct phase in the life course did not exist in the Middle Ages; she also refutes the claim made by Shorter (1976) that mothers did not really start to love and nurture their children until modern times. Ariès in particular is seen as basing his general theorization too heavily on noble and propertied families. Pollock argues, in a vein very similar to contemporary critics of theories of individualization:

> The sources upon which the received view is founded are obviously suspect and are certainly not a sound enough base to warrant the grand theories which have been derived from them. Aspects of the thesis, especially the assertion that there was no concept of childhood, have been shown by later research to be completely unjustified. (1988: 52)

Pollock also makes the point that most of the grand theorists she criticizes have tried to explain the history of childhood in relation to other trends in society, for example the growth of education, social welfare, democracy and even individualism. Thus she perceives a top-down approach in which developments in childhood are interpreted as fitting with other larger and over-determining trends. In this way family relationships are 'read off' from other events and their course is seen to be inevitably in tune with other social forces. Such a reading is possible only if the interiority of these relationships is given cursory attention, while signs of congruence with broad theoretical explanations are treated as sufficient supporting evidence.

The longest-running debate over the family so far, the fourth and last under consideration here, is the contention that the family is in decline, a contention often supported by social statistics on divorce, lone motherhood and births out of wedlock (Wright and Jagger, 1999). The counter-position or rejection of this thesis is based on different readings of social trends and/or by arguments based on intensive empirical research, acknowledging that some families are changing in structure but suggesting that they still provide love and support for family members and kin (Lewis, 2001; Williams, 2004). It is clear that the decline argument has its roots in the earlier debate about the shift from extended families to nuclear families. This foundational argument sets the tone for understanding modern families, which are seen as inadequately connected with kin and thus unable or unwilling to take on the proper role of caring for kin and creating the right multi-generational context in which children can be raised. In this sense, for the pessimists at least, the modern family is always already lacking desirable qualities. But this baseline argument has been strengthened by specific interpretations of the rise in divorce rates, patterns of serial monogamy, illegitimacy rates and so on. Thus, for example, trends towards more heterosexual cohabitation are understood to signify a rejection not just of marriage but also of moral values, which involves avoiding the responsibilities that should attend creating a new family unit. High divorce rates are also interpreted as a flight from responsibility, a refusal to work sufficiently hard at relationships and a prizing of individual happiness over collective – or more specifically – children's well-being. Such arguments have been particularly strong in the US (e.g. Popenoe, 1993; Blankenhorn et al., eds, 1990; Etzioni, 1993) but have also had a voice in the UK (e.g. Dennis and Erdos, 1993; Dench, 1997; Morgan, 1995). From time to time the feminist movement has been identified as the cause of family decline (Berger and Berger, 1983; Dench, 1997), at other times it has been men's fecklessness (Ehrenreich, 1983; Dennis and Erdos, 1993). But the overall reason, from this viewpoint, appears to be seen as the growth of individualism and the prioritizing of the selfish self over the needs of others.

As Jane Lewis has pointed out, the interpretation in favour of decline has rested much weight on social statistics while also being politically compelling:

> Much of the debate about the family in the late twentieth century has in fact been a struggle over the meaning of the statistics, with little attempt to refer to the admittedly limited research on the changes that have actually taken place inside family relationships, or to investigate them further. However, simple assertions as to the power of selfish individualism have had a significant effect on policy making on both sides of the Atlantic. (2001: 11)

Lewis's reference to the 'admittedly limited research' on changes going on inside family relationships is not entirely accurate. The minimal influence of small-scale research seems to have less to do with how much of this research is available than the fact that it is perceived to be less 'useful' than survey-based research. Small-scale empirical projects are inevitably local and specific – indeed that is their strength, both epistemologically and analytically – but this approach is rarely seen as relevant to national policy making.

Attempts to refute the decline thesis have been around almost as long as the thesis itself. Ronald Fletcher (1966, orig. 1962), in a generally optimistic appraisal of social change in Britain after the Second World War, saw the family as becoming more democratic and felt it was increasingly founded upon good-quality intimate relationships between spouses:

> In the modern marriage, both partners choose each other freely as persons. Both are of equal status and expect to have an equal share in

taking decisions and in pursuing their sometimes mutual, sometimes separate and diverse, tastes and interests. They live together permanently and intimately in their own home and in relative independence of wider groups of kindred. (1966: 130)

Indeed, he argued that the rising divorce rate was indicative of people's high expectations of marriage and their refusal to put up with the kinds of situations families had been forced to tolerate in the past. Throughout his book he strove to compare the modern family and its benefits with the deprivations and hardships of families in former times. His book is therefore on a completely different trajectory to those that focus on decline. Michael Young and Peter Willmott (1987, orig. 1957) took an equally benign view of family life and also managed to identify through empirical research how extended family networks continued to work notwithstanding social change. They too focused on growing equality and democracy in heterosexual relationships in marriage, ultimately proposing that the family was becoming symmetrical (Willmott and Young, 1973). Later arguments against the decline of the family have appeared in the US (Bengtson et al., 2002; Stacey, 1996) and in the UK (Williams, 2004; Silva and Smart, eds, 1999; Lewis, 2001; Brannen et al., 2004) and these studies have tended to emphasize – or at least recognize – continuity and connectedness across family members. In the main these studies have been based on in-depth interviews that examine not only living arrangements but also a range of family practices and the meanings attached to forms of exchange and connectedness which tend not to be visible at the national survey level. The incorporation of the meanings people themselves give to their relationships has been a particularly important element in these alternative studies because, as suggested by Lewis (quoted above), with survey data the researcher often has to impute or guess the reasons for visible trends, while the qualitative researcher is more able to include the complex, contradictory and changing reasons that people have for behaving as they do.

Alongside the development of a stronger body of research derived from qualitative interview methods, there has also grown up a reappraisal of family life as lived and experienced during what is often perceived as the 'Golden Age' (whether located in the 1950s or sometimes in the Victorian and Edwardian eras). The essay by Joanne Klein (2005) on unorthodox working-class domestic life between 1900 and 1939 shows detailed understanding of how even respectable working classes, in this case policemen in Liverpool, Birmingham and Manchester, could have very irregular marriages. Although divorce was rare, she found evidence of men simply moving in with other women and sometimes even refusing to maintain their first wives and children. She argues that:

> Police records indicate that flexible notions of marriage persisted with the working class much longer than previously assumed, not disappearing by the later nineteenth century but lasting into the interwar era. The legal limitations of marriage did not hamper the pursuit of domestic happiness. While only a small minority of policemen lived in unusual situations, their more conventional colleagues had few problems with their choices. Even senior officers showed remarkable tolerance for domestic irregularities. (2005: 211)

Equally the detailed work of family historians (for example Davidoff et al., 1999 and Bailey, 2003) puts a different complexion on the rather rosy contemporary vision of the supposedly contented and dutiful families of the past. The more empirical research there is, especially of the historical variety, the more it seems that the Golden Age of the family is a cultural myth which is used discursively to criticize various aspects of contemporary life. As Peter Laslett (2005, orig. 1965) stated, in his insistence upon a 'proper understanding of ourselves': 'The wish to believe in the large, extended kin-enfolding, multi-generational, welfare- and support-providing household in the world we have lost seems to be exceedingly difficult to expose to critical evaluation' (2005: 92). In other words, there seem to be strong reasons for keeping myths about family life in times passed alive, regardless of empirical evidence. This should alert us to the extent to which, in dealing with families, we are dealing with aspirations, yearnings, falsehoods and nostalgia, and this is emotive territory.

Engagement with the individualization thesis

Having outlined some of the core areas of debate in the field of family life, I now turn to the most recent site of contention, which is the debate over individualization (sometimes known as de-traditionalization) and what it means for family life and relationships. The individualization thesis has become the 'big idea' in this area, both building on and superseding previous great debates. Such ideas, as Clifford Geertz (2000, orig. 1985) has pointed out, can become hugely popular and are seized upon as if they can suddenly explain everything and throw an illuminating light all around. But, he continues:

> After we have become familiar with the new idea [. . .], after it has become part of our general stock of theoretical concepts, our expectations are brought more into balance with its actual uses, and its excessive popularity is ended. A few zealots persist in the old key-to-the-universe view of it; but less driven thinkers settle down after a while to the problems the idea has really generated. They try to apply it and extend it where it applies and where it is capable of extension; and they desist where it does not apply or cannot be extended. (2000: 3–4)

This seems to be where we have arrived with the individualization thesis and there have been many challenges to its claims over the last decade (Jamieson, 1998, 1999; Ribbens McCarthy, 2003; Smart and Shipman, 2004; Brannen and Nilsen, 2005; Gross, 2005; Duncan and Smith, 2006; Crow, 2002; Lewis, 2001). This is in the main because there is such a lack of congruence between the depiction of contemporary family life in the work of individualization theorists and the kinds of lives being represented in local and more closely specified studies of families, kinship and friendship networks. It is important to enter a caveat, however, because not all of those who might be fitted into the individualization group offer the same explanations and neither do all the critics reject everything that the individualization theorists argue.

Elisabeth Beck-Gernsheim defines the individualization thesis as having two components:

> On the one hand, the traditional social relationships, bonds and belief systems that used to determine people's lives in the narrowest detail have been losing more and more of their meaning. [. . .] New space and new options have thereby opened up for individuals. Now men and women can and should, may and must, decide for themselves how to shape their lives – within certain limits, at least.
>
>   On the other hand, individualization means that people are linked into [social] institutions [. . .]. These institutions produce various regulations [. . .] that are typically addressed to individuals rather than the family as a whole. And the crucial feature of these new regulations is that they enjoin the individual to lead a life of his or her own beyond any ties to the family or other groups – or sometimes even to shake off such ties and to act without referring to them. (2002: ix)

What seems surprising about this definition is that it proceeds as if all the previous debates on family change had never happened. While the idea of tradition is evoked, no specificity is provided so the reader cannot be sure if this passage refers to the pre-industrial era, the Victorian era or the early twentieth century. The idea that during this vague period people slavishly followed the prevalent rules and dominant beliefs is accepted without hesitation. A special moment in history having been created, that moment can then be compared with the present which, by dint of such a contrast, looks challengingly different. But the past in this representation is little more than a straw man devised for the sake of argument.

The second element in Beck-Gernsheim's definition relies upon the standard way in which sociology has understood family change to happen only in reaction to (larger, more important) changes elsewhere. Thus there is the premise that because social institutions change (employment, welfare, education, law), there will be inescapable pressure on families to change in line with their needs. She predicts that individuals will necessarily respond to the new calls being made of them, and that the family will be transformed as a result.

Although Beck-Gernsheim is uncertain of exactly what the future will bring, the whole tenor of this work and her work with

Ulrich Beck (Beck and Beck-Gernsheim 1995, 2002) is extremely pessimistic. The reader is left in no doubt that the future for the family is bleak and that modern social conditions will succeed in pulling families apart. In *The Normal Chaos of Love* Beck and Beck-Gernsheim focus on the push-pull features of the process of individualization. In other words, they point to the changes which are pushing families apart (mainly divorce, women's paid employment, equality, demands for flexibility and mobility in labour markets); they also suggest that this atomization of individuals in their various life trajectories produces a reaction in the form of a yearning for love and stable relationships. While this might explain why the desire to get married and have children remains strong, they go on to point out that there is no structural basis to sustain such relationships. On the contrary all the social forces seem designed to ensure they fail. They state:

> This finding is both paradoxical and mysterious: the family is simultaneously disintegrating and being put on a pedestal. If one can draw conclusions about beliefs from how people behave, seventh heaven and mental torment seem to be very close neighbours in our ideal image of a loving couple. Perhaps they just live in different storeys – tower room and torture chamber – in the same castle. [. . .] What induces the sexes to tear at each other's throats and still keep their high hopes of finding true love and personal fulfilment with this partner, or the next, setting standards which are so high that disappointment is almost inevitable? (1995: 173)

In *Individualization* (2002), Beck and Beck-Gernsheim elaborate on the ways in which the process of individualization requires a 'staging of everyday life' because so much co-ordination is required to keep individual biographies and life projects from pulling apart. Thus decisions (large and small) are constantly being made because people can no longer rely on following old rules and models. And it is ultimately in the requirement constantly to negotiate and bargain that instability (apparently) lurks: relationships become 'thinner and more fragile' (2002: 97) because they depend on personal co-operation. For Beck the family is a 'zombie category' (2002: 204), by which he appears to mean that the family is dead even if people live their lives as if it were still alive. This kind of provocative statement is typical of Beck and Beck-Gernsheim's work, which often produces an enigmatic quality. While the use of dramatic style, polemical crescendos and rhetorical questions makes their writing distinctive, it can also make the meaning opaque. To some extent it is possible to superimpose one's own meaning on their work and this may be why their contribution has been so apparently influential. They deal with issues of contemporary importance, their themes are topical and relevant, but ultimately it is hard to grasp the substance and direction of their argument although its pessimistic tenor remains unmistakable.

In much the same vein, and definitely on the pessimistic end of the continuum, is the work of Zygmunt Bauman, who appears almost to have an apocalyptic vision of contemporary families and relationships. There is no ambiguity in his work that the perceived shift away from 'given' and fixed kinship systems, towards (elective) kinship of affinity, is a bad thing:

> The falling out of fashion and out of practice of orthodox affinity cannot but rebound on the plight of kinship. Lacking stable bridges for inflowing traffic, kinship networks feel frail and threatened. The boundaries are blurred and disputed, they dissolve in a terrain with no clear-cut property titles and hereditary tenures – a frontier-land; sometimes a battlefield, other times an object of court battles that are no less bitter. Kinship networks cannot be sure of their chances of survival, let alone calculate their life expectations. (2003: 31)

Bauman's ideas run directly counter to most empirical sociological studies of family and kinship in Britain and he offers no evidence in support of his assertions. Yet his work, along with that of Beck and Beck-Gernsheim, seems to have captured a cultural Zeitgeist in which increasing despair about families is on the verge of becoming conventional wisdom.[5] I return to the issue of the power of this kind of theorizing below because, if it is largely devoid of empirical support, I do not think it can simply be dismissed. So at this point I turn to the more positive versions of the individualization theses.

Giddens (1992) is often placed in the same category as Beck and Beck-Gernsheim, notwithstanding the clear differences between their arguments (Crow, 2002; Smart and Neale, 1999). In his view of 'progress' and the positive improvements that are being achieved in heterosexual relationships, he follows more in the tradition of Ronald Fletcher. Moreover, he is keenly aware of the significance of same-sex relationships, which he sees as leading the way in terms of creating more democratic styles of relating. Beck and Beck-Gernsheim seem not to have noticed the increasing visibility of same-sex households and do not include these relationships in their discussions of love and family life. For Giddens it is precisely the ability to redefine relationships and to be 'free' of traditional, status-bound chains of obligation that gives rise to greater democracy and equality in relationships. While he sees equality as transforming gender relationships in (potentially) positive ways, he recognizes that this is not happening in a straightforward manner. Beck and Beck-Gernsheim, on the other hand, see precisely the lure of unattainable equality in families as the reason for the greatest conflict and disappointment. They assert, quite simply, that the family cannot be an egalitarian institution – if equality is desired, the family must be abandoned.[6] Giddens's work on relationships has become best known for its development of the ideas of confluent love and the pure relationship. By 'pure relationship' he means: 'a social relationship [which] is entered into for its own sake, for what can be derived by each person from a sustained association with another; and which is continued only in so far as it is thought by both parties to deliver enough satisfactions for each individual to stay within it' (1992: 58). And he explains confluent love as 'active, contingent love, [which] therefore jars with the "for-ever", "one-and-only" qualities of the romantic love complex' (1992: 61).

These two concepts are used to distinguish the defining characteristics of contemporary relationships when compared with the forms that (hetero)sexual relationships took in previous times. Giddens has been adversely criticized in his account of contemporary relationships for ignoring the on-going significance of social class, gender inequality, power and intergenerational relationships (Jamieson, 1999; Crow, 2002; Ribbens McCarthy and Edwards, 2002; Smart and Neale, 1999). The individuals who inhabit his landscapes seem remarkably well resourced and free from economic and/or social constraints. As Crow points out, in his defence against such criticisms Giddens argues that he is discussing an 'ideal' form of family/relationship and one which may come about in the future. Crow finds this an inadequate response. But the debate does raise the issue of the scope and purpose of such anticipatory theorizing and whether literal readings are always the most fruitful or generous way of assessing the value of the ideas – an issue I discuss below.

It is clear that some sociologists have found Giddens's work useful, particularly in their research on same-sex relationships (Weeks et al., 2001) or on new trends in living and relating which are beyond the notion of the family (Roseneil and Budgeon, 2004). His emphasis on the freeing up of space in relationships to create different forms and to have different expectations appears to have struck a chord. It can be argued that his emphasis on negotiation and choice both builds on existing work (Finch and Mason, 1993) and prefigures some of the issues raised by Ray Pahl and David Pevalin (2005) in their analysis of friendship and the continuum between friends and family.[7] In spite of all the adverse criticism, Giddens has provided a kind of platform for new ways of thinking about families and his work has not been entirely divorced from the findings of more empirical sociology.

This brings us to the question of the purpose and usefulness of grand theorizing in the field of family life and intimacy. Hostility towards grand statements and generalizations about changes to family life seems to have been mounting since the mid-1990s and it is important to consider whether this reflects an antipathy to more theoretical work in general, or simply a discomfort with the popularity of ideas which are poorly conceived and which ignore competing evidence. Julia Brannen and Ann Nilsen (2005) are clear that they have no antipathy towards theorizing *per se* but they suggest that it needs to arise in a grounded way from empirical research. They also make it clear that there is a problem for the discipline altogether if some ideas (which have little support in the research community) are taken up at a political level and enter into everyday perceptions. But it is important to separate the strands of some of these issues. After addressing the issue of political popularity and the ways in which ideas about changing commitment or possibly even the disintegration of family life have been taken up, I conclude this chapter by looking at the problems of grand theorizing.

It seems that the preparedness of politicians and the media to pick up and exaggerate accounts of the 'decline' of family life predates the rise of contemporary theories of individualization. Moreover, as Denise Riley (1983) notably argued in relation to John Bowlby's theories of maternal deprivation, the relationship between academic theories, politics and policies is far from simple or direct. Riley took issue with the tendency in feminist work to 'blame' Bowlby for pushing mothers back into the home after the Second World War because his theories about the harm befalling infants and children who were deprived of their mothers' care while living in institutions were 'used' as a rationale for closing nurseries. Riley documented the ways in which Bowlby's work was simplified and used selectively, but she also pointed to the other reasons for the closure of the nurseries, including the fact that mothers did not like the quality of care they offered. Her work is a kind of cautionary tale which warns us against simply blaming social theorists for the popularity of their ideas. The work of Giddens and Beck and Beck-Gernsheim certainly reflects a contemporary cultural Zeitgeist about individual agency and choice, and we might argue that they should be more critically self-reflexive, but rather than causing the current belief in the loss of altruism in family life and the decline of commitment, they seem to be reflecting it somewhat uncritically. According to Brannen and Nilsen (2005), this uncritical regurgitation of populist thinking is inappropriate to the intellectual character of sociology, but this is different from being critical of these social theorists because their ideas have resonated in political and policy circles.

On the topic of whether there is a place for grand or generalizing theories, Simon Duncan and Darren Smith for example argue:

> There are severe problems with [. . .] these almost millenarian visions of contemporary society, for all their value as heuristic devices – they are not well founded in terms of empirical and historical evidence, they lack reliable methodologies, and they pay inadequate attention to stabilities and continuities as well as change. They are also top-down, abstract visions with little connection to particular social contexts. This suggests that the epochal sense of family transformation often claimed may not be warranted. (2006: 2–3)

While these are well-founded criticisms, the question is whether we should reject some of the current theorizing around family life because it is of poor quality, or whether family researchers are starting to reject this kind of theorization altogether. The two notable phrases in the above passage are 'heuristic device' and 'abstract vision'. Duncan and Smith seem to think that heuristic devices can have a value; it is just that they need to be well founded. Abstract visions, however, appear to have no merit. Yet heuristic devices are rarely well founded in the sense that scientific findings might be; they are actually more like suggestive metaphors. Equally visions are often abstract – perhaps always so – but this does not mean that they may not be useful in terms of opening up new ways of addressing 'old' problems or of generating new fields of enquiry. It may be that the individualization thesis is a poor example of grand or generalizing theory, but it may be unwise to throw the baby out with the bathwater. As Jennifer Mason (2002; orig. 1996) has usefully pointed out, there are different ways of creating ideas with data, for example arguing evocatively or reflexively. In some instances evocation may be the primary way to generate understandings precisely because one is dealing with feelings or intangible issues. Thus researchers are not simply dealing with evidence, nor are they interpreting the given world, they are making meanings through a number of different ways of using data. Mason (2002: 182) cautions against losing creativity and inspiration by reducing theory construction to one type of process, namely treating data simply as evidence.

Individualization theorists have injected debate and excitement into the field of families, intimacy and relationships in a way achieved by feminist theories some twenty or thirty years previously. Many of the theories that were debated then were criticized in the same way as individualization theorists are now, particularly in relation to the tendency to generalize. But the debate generated more empirical work and a greater refinement of ideas. So, while I agree in almost every detail with the criticisms made by Duncan and Smith, Brannen and Nilsen, and most of the other detractors of the individualization thesis (including my own work), it would be a mistake to rob the field of its visions and its heuristic devices. The problem of relying solely on empirical research to generate knowledge and theories is that it is inevitably linked to the past and/or the present and reflects the scope of expressible experience. Moreover, our existing method-ologies may be rigorous but they may not always be sufficiently inno-vative to grasp everything that might matter to people in families, relationships and intimacies. We might therefore be rejecting ways of knowing and ways of imagining if we insist that the only useful the-ories are grounded theories based on specific empirical studies. One has only to think about the significance of feminist theories in the 1980s which pre-dated most social research on gender relations in households, or about the re-conceptualization by Michel Foucault (1979, French orig. 1976) of the workings of power, or the imagi-native leap by Morgan (1996) from understanding family as an insti-tution to seeing it as a range of flexible practices. All of these ideas have seeped into our 'ways of seeing' – to borrow John Berger's seminal book title of 1972 – and have facilitated different ways of both generating and interpreting empirical data. So the relationship between theorizing and empirical work can take different forms and need not be a direct one as is implied in the idea of grounded theory. Moreover, theory can operate at a range of levels and the fact that at its most general it inevitably becomes imprecise does not mean that the broad canvas does not provide a way of conceptualizing large-scale trends or even of linking together ideas and explanations devel-oped at a micro- or meso-level. Problems only really arise when such theorizations cannot respond to the weight of counter-evidence which is generated by more local or precise studies or by more thoughtful theoretical contributions.

One example of how the individualization thesis can be refined, rejecting what is useful but incorporating the kind of knowledge and understandings generated by empirical research, is provided by Neil Gross (2005). He argues that theorists of de-traditionalization (or individualization) have misunderstood that there are different components of tradition. He agrees with them that what he calls 'regulative traditions' have declined, by which he means those con-straints that reinforced arrangements such as life-long, gender-differentiated heterosexual marriage. This means that people do not have to live in such traditional ways, but he continues:

> That there is some evidence that this tradition is in decline, however, does not mean that reflexivity, understood as unbounded agency and

creativity, has rushed in to fill the void. This is so because social action is also shaped by what I call 'meaning-constitutive traditions', which involve patterns of sense making passed down from one generation to the next. (2005: 288)

Gross goes on to argue that this element of tradition imposes cultural constraints which in turn means that people's behaviour may not be radically different, or they may carry forward similar values (to those of their parents/communities) even if they are living a slightly different life style (Bengtson et al., 2002, and Lewis, 2001). He stresses the importance of intersubjectively shared traditions and also the influence of sedimented habituality which, taken together, mean that the individual is not a free agent, but embedded in culture and history, with these qualities manifesting themselves through forms of everyday behaviour which are not radically different to social action in the past. Gross's way of re-theorizing de-traditionalization meets many of the points raised by Brannen and Nilsen and also Duncan and Smith, whose empirical research reveals traces of conventional lives and also fairly conventional expectations as far as intimacy and relationships are concerned. In this way Gross offers a complex way of understanding both continuity and change, which is linked neither with stories of decline, nor with radical changes to values of commitment and care in families and across generations. Before pursuing the themes of connectedness and relationality, which have so far been given too little consideration in theories of individualization, I now return to the ideas that go towards constituting a different vision of families and relationships, namely the proposed field of personal life.

Towards a conception of a different field: personal life

Ever since the interventions of feminist scholarship into the area of families, the private sphere, domestic life and gender relationships, the term 'family' has been rendered problematic. Michèle Barrett and Mary McIntosh (1982) mounted one of the most sustained critiques of the term, identifying it as a form of ideology rather than a descriptive concept, and one which sustained women's subordination while deflecting discontent through appeals to the naturalness of the biological unit of the heterosexual couple and their children. Following this, feminist work not only tried to avoid using the word family, but to strip away the ideological veil that shrouded discussions of families by deploying more neutral terms such as 'household' or 'private sphere'. There was also a body of empirical research which focused on abuses, violence and economic inequality in nuclear families. Following on from such approaches other criticisms were developed, in particular from the viewpoint of same-sex households; in the UK this included reaction to a notorious legal provision which prevented schools from teaching children about 'pretended families' (same-sex relationships) (Weeks, 1991). The grossness of depicting gay and lesbian households as 'pretended' families led to an absolute aversion to the term. However, the concept of families (as opposed to 'the' family) seemed incredibly tenacious and not only refused to be banished from the lexicon, but seemed instead to expand quite happily to include a range of relationships and households which would never have fitted the original sociological definition of a nuclear family. Thus concepts developed of families of choice (Weston, 1991) or of friends as family (Pahl, 2000) and, although a core notion of family has undoubtedly remained (especially in relation to close biological kin), the term seems to have become more inclusive and more generous in its embrace. David Morgan (1996) has also helped to shift the field conceptually through his development of the idea of family practices, which captures the idea that families are what families do, no longer being defined exclusively by co-residence or even ultimately by kinship and marriage.

The field is therefore going through a very interesting phase as the sociological imagination stretches and reconfigures in order better to grasp and reflect the complexities of contemporary personal life. And this brings me precisely to the concept of 'personal life', a term now increasingly applied to include not only families as conventionally conceived, but also newer family forms and relationships, reconfigured kinship networks, and friendships. But as suggested at the start of this chapter, 'personal life' is intended to be more than a terminological holdall. The terminology of personal life seeks to embrace conceptual shifts as well as empirical changes to social realities and, for the sake of clarity, I shall enumerate the main components of this field before turning to some of its limitations.

1   First, it is vital to specify what is meant by 'personal'. The term is used in contradistinction to 'individual' because of the problems identified above both with understandings of the individualization thesis and with atomized or disconnected individualism. 'The personal' designates an area of life which impacts closely on people and means much to them, but which does not presume that there is an autonomous individual who makes free choices and exercises unfettered agency. This means that the term 'personal life' can invoke the social, indeed it is conceptualized as always already part of the social. This is because the very possibility of personal life is predicated upon a degree of self-reflection and also connectedness with others. Just as George Herbert Mead (1967, orig. 1934) posited the distinction between the 'I' and the 'me' (where the 'I' is the agentic ego and the 'me' is the social, interconnected person), so I suggest that the field of personal life is the 'me' compared with the 'I' of the individualization thesis. To live a personal life is to have agency and to make choices, but the personhood implicit in the concept requires the presence of others to respond to and to contextualize those actions and choices. Personal life is a reflexive state, but it is not private and it is lived out in relation to one's class position, ethnicity, gender and so on.

2   The idea that personal life is embedded in the social (and cultural, legal, economic etc.) is an analytical statement. It does not mean that ordinary people use the term in colloquial speech in that way, nor does it mean that they always necessarily have a conscious awareness of the social which frames their specific personal lives (Mills, 1940; Brannen and Nilsen, 2005). But the sociologist can map personal lives (revealed through the research process) into their social context and into their specific history or spatial location.

3   The concept of personal life allows for ideas of the life project – particularly significant in the work of Giddens and Beck – in

which people have scope for decisions and plans, but it does not incorporate the idea of individually crafted biographies as if people are free-floating agents with sufficient resources to achieve their goals. In Gross's terms 'meaning-constitutive traditions' are important here, as are such structural factors as social class, ethnicity and gender. So this mode of conceptualizing recognizes the importance of memory and generation or cultural transmission and is alert to the extent to which people are embedded in both sedimented structures and the imaginary.

4   The term is also appropriately neutral in that it does not prioritize relationships with biological kin or marital bonds. Such a landscape of personal life does not have hierarchical boundaries between friends and kin. This means that there is more open conceptual space for families of choice, same-sex intimacies, reconfigured kinship formations and so on.

5   Of particular significance is the way in which the concept contains within it a sense of motion. Personal life is never still or stationary in the way that the old idea of 'the family' appeared to be. While the concept of the life course has injected movement into studies of family life, this adds only a social dimension of generational and cohort ageing, whereas it is equally important to capture other kinds of motion. For example unemployment or divorce can transform personal life, often affecting income, housing and well-being and shifting people into completely different places and spaces, yet these common occurrences are not conceptualized as part of the life course.

6   There is also the potential to overcome the older distinctions made between private and public spheres which have conceptualized family life as a distinct place or institution separate from other social spaces and structures. Personal life is lived in many different places and spaces, it is cumulative (through memory, history and the passage of time) and it forms a range of connections, thus making it flexible rather than brittle and breakable. So personal life is not so concerned with boundary marking and provides the possibility of tracing its flows through systems of education, or work, or elsewhere.

7   The concept also gives recognition to those areas of life which used to be slightly below the sociological radar. Thus personal

life includes issues of sexuality, bodies, emotions, intimacy and can bring them together, creating a whole that is greater than its parts, rather than treating them as separate subfields of the sociological discipline.

8   Finally, personal life as a concept does not invoke the white, middle-class, heterosexual family in the way that, historically at least, the concept of 'the family' has. This means that important dimensions of class, ethnicity, religion, sexuality, gender, and disability can be written through the narrative and given significance through attentiveness not only to difference but by reference to cultural tradition, habitus, memories, generational transmission and emotion. This is not to imply that all these elements can or should be achieved all the time but shifting away from the dominant concept of the family to this broader sphere of social and emotional (inter)relationships opens up new conceptual configurations.

These points are suggestive of the value of reconfiguring the field. But this does not mean that terms such as 'family' or 'family life' should be banned or that the notions of kinship and friendship should be collapsed into a formless sludge. These ideas about personal life are intended to provide a conceptual orientation and potential toolbox rather than a rigid, rule-bound manifesto. Among the inevitable limitations with the concept, the most obvious is that its scope can be seen as too wide and it can appear to include anything and everything that pertains to a person. With more traditional concepts such as the family there were clear conceptual boundaries between 'it' and other institutions. But the comfort achieved by having conceptual boundaries has been at the cost of misrepresenting the ways in which personal life is lived and there are increasing demands for an understanding of fluidity. Morgan (1996) addressed this problem in the development of his ideas about family practices. He argues that 'a growing sense of fluidity' is apparent in a range of sociological fields such that the previously discrete areas of 'family', 'work', 'leisure' and so on are not sealed off from one another. Rather Morgan suggests that one might start at a given point, but will inevitably cross over these other spaces. He deploys the metaphor of the kaleidoscope with 'the emphasis on shifting patterns of relationships' (1996: 187) to express the kind of realities that sociology seeks to represent and understand. He states:

> The notion of 'family practices' was elaborated to convey a sense of flow and movement between a whole set of overlapping social practices, practices which were both constructed by the observer and lived by the actual practitioners. Thus 'family', in this account [of family practices], is not a thing but a way of looking at, and describing, practices which might also be described in a variety of other ways. (1996: 199)

Morgan's family practices are therefore fairly unbounded. By inference the idea of personal life is broader still as it does not keep the term 'family' at its core; it is thus an extension of Morgan's original thinking, only slightly wider in scope.

Work still remains to be done on theorizing the meshing and threading of personal life with the spaces of work life, cultural life or political life. Research on emotions in the work place is acknowledging, for example, that strands of personal life weave their way through zones which are meant to be free of such things (Fineman, ed., 2000). Equally, work on the embodied nature of social class (Skeggs, 1997) and the moral implications of class (Sayer, 2005) reveal the significance of both personal experiences and feelings to a better sociological understanding of social inequalities. Work on memory and life histories too provide for ways of acknowledging the significance of the personal to the social. Making these connections will be a vital part of establishing how useful the idea of a conceptual field of personal life might be to the broader sociological enterprise. However, there are important stages in this larger process which need to be addressed first. In the next chapter I therefore turn to a more substantial discussion of what I see as undervalued but core elements of the field, ideas developed through engagement with work around memory, emotions, love, unhappiness and anxiety, connectedness and cultural transmission, family secrets and the significance of material things to emotional and relational life.

2

The Cultural Turn in the Sociology of Family Life

Fiona Devine and Mike Savage begin their essay on the cultural turn in the sociological analysis of class as follows:

> It is widely recognised that the discipline of sociology, especially in the UK, has been profoundly affected by the 'cultural turn' in recent years. Not only has the study of culture become a significant area of sociological research, but key debates now explore the cultural dimensions of a variety of economic, social and political processes. (2005: 1)

In so doing they make an important distinction between the sociology of culture and the exploration of cultural dimensions in fields normally thought to be quite separate from the cultural. The sociology of culture (often including fashion, consumption, media, literature and art) has developed as a subfield of the discipline since the 1980s, but what has become more interesting has been the recognition of the embeddedness of culture in, for example, work-place practices or most particularly social class. As Devine and Savage acknowledge, it is not that there was no recognition of these factors in earlier studies of class: indeed, issues such as class identity and class consciousness were often discussed. However, these were often mechanistically read off from a set of theoretical presumptions about how they should work. It was not really until the contribution of Pierre Bourdieu (1977, French orig. 1972) that a more sensitive theorization of the culture of class and its embodied nature led to a recognition of how important a cultural analysis might be, especially in explaining the persistence of class differentiation and signs of class difference (Ray and Sayer, eds, 1999; Skeggs, 1997). So the 'cultural turn' to which Devine and Savage refer is significant in its impact on the discipline rather than being an extension of the discipline. New issues can now be considered and incorporated; what were formerly peripheral issues or simply 'noise' can become central. Interestingly, this cultural turn occurred somewhat earlier in feminist work (Bradley and Fenton, 1999; Barrett, 1992; Roseneil, 1995) but perhaps only when cultural analysis really reached the core of the discipline – namely social class – was the full impact recognized. So using this broad approach this chapter explores the extent to which a 'cultural turn' can be identified in the field of family and intimacy.[1] Among the range of theorists to have entered the field, there does not appear to be one figure as influential as Bourdieu in terms of the analysis of social class, but there are a range of important contributions which, taken together, may be transforming the way this area can be understood.

Making the turn in 'family studies'

There is evidence that studies of families, relationships and kinship are beginning to incorporate new ways of thinking. As outlined in chapter 1, the work of David Morgan (1996) captures a move away from perceiving family as an institution towards mapping family practices (and seeing families as constituted by what they do). This conceptual shift was a vital stage in 'freeing' the ways we think about family life and living. In addition the work of Janet Finch and Jennifer Mason (1993, 2000), which has insisted on talking about kinship (and reconceptualizing kinship) while most studies of family life focus almost exclusively on households or parent/child, has tried to stretch the narrow ways in which sociologists think about how we relate to our 'relatives' and whom we choose to include in our spheres of intimacy. In other discipline areas too there is evidence of new ways of conceptualizing. Perhaps it is most apparent in anthropology which now talks definitively about the new anthropology of kinship (Carsten, 2004), which has been brought about through at least three routes: the rejection of traditional structuralist thinking, the influence of feminist work and the fresh challenges to understanding kinship wrought by the advent of new reproductive technologies. There are longer-standing traces of these new forms of thinking too. The semi-autobiographical works of the cultural historian Carolyn Steedman (1986, 1992) and the film studies analyst Annette Kuhn (1995) point to the significance of memory, place and history in understanding the workings of family life (in both the present and the past). Yet while these books were taken up in feminist studies, they were almost completely ignored in the more mainstream sociology of the family. In the area of social history too, the work of John Gillis (1996, 2004) has contributed to important insights into the ways in which families inhabit both personal and cultural imaginaries and has explored the relationship between these two. Gillis's work is gradually being acknowledged outside cultural history and with it comes increased comprehension of the significance of the past for an appreciation of the present. His focus on cultural memory and practices/rituals that support these memories has brought sociology closer to recognizing the importance of everyday activities and the realm of the imagined. The significance of place, hence the home, through to a recognition of the material culture of family living is also being gradually appreciated (see chapter 7). This comes from autobiography and visual analysis (particularly the emphasis on family albums), as well as from the anthropology of everyday life (Chapman and Hockey, eds, 1999; Miller, ed., 1998).

The cultural turn, which is in process, is therefore reliant on themes which already exist but which have not been brought together coherently before. What is more, the topics that these varied authors address are more salient to a lay audience than some of the typical concerns of a fairly standard sociology of the family. What matters to most ordinary people is likely to be whether they can make their new house or flat feel like home, whether the bequests in their unmarried aunt's will are fairly distributed, or whether their family secrets will leak out when their children go to school. Of course, sociology has never taken as an imperative that it should direct its gaze exclusively or predominantly towards what matters to people, yet it seems strange that so much of what matters in everyday family life has sparked so little interest in the discipline. There are resonances here with the struggle that Ann Oakley faced in 1974 when she published *The Sociology of Housework*. At the time housework was beneath the radar of the lofty theoretical concerns of sociology, not just because it was women's work but because it was commonplace. What mattered, sociologically speaking, was seen to occur on departure from the domestic sphere, not within it. Feminist work in the 1970s and 1980s challenged this view and argued for more interest in and research into gender relationships (e.g. Pahl, 1980; Dobash and Dobash, 1980; Delphy and Leonard, 1992). But this body of work, vital though it was, tended to con-ceptualize family life in terms of (unequal) domestic relations or as economic exchanges within households. These analyses were not the whole story and there remained a gap between what was seen as the domain of sociology (relations of power, structures and pat-terns of family life, the reproduction of class, gender and minority statuses) and the domain of psychology (child development, dys-functional relationships, the measurement of gender difference). Through this gap fell certain events, ranging from the kinds of ritual that people followed at Christmas, Diwali or Hanukkah, through the significance attached to traditional family holidays or reunions, to other landmarks in family life – the arguments that often sur-round weddings and funerals; the workings of complex webs of sensitive relationships; dealing with missed loved ones; anticipating the death of a parent; or the burden of keeping secret one's sexual-ity for fear of causing distress. This list is far from exhaustive, but it is indicative of the kinds of issue that are part of everyday family life yet which, as used to be the case with housework, still generally sit outside the framework of sociological interest.

It might be argued that just because such events are part of every-day life it does not necessarily follow that they are of equal interest to everyone, whether lay person or academic. Yet these are bread and butter topics for magazine stories, television and radio soaps and fiction. They are also the stuff of gossip, which used to generate some sociological interest (e.g. Frankenberg, 1957) although the focus then was on the ways in which gossip created conformity in the community. Gossip as a process of sharing experiences or even of expressing diversity in family living has been largely ignored by sociologists. Moreover, there has been a huge rise in interest in family lineage among ordinary people (as opposed to local or family historians); such attempts to capture an understanding of the past through people unmet yet personally meaningful show the work-ings of an active family imaginary in the population at large. People appear to be using the past to make sense of their present; they wish not only to understand past processes, but also, at a more mundane level, to see whether they are 'like' their forebears and ancestors. These new hobbies and pastimes have a cultural meaning, suggest-ing an interiority to relationships which sociology is only just beginning to acknowledge and explore.

One of the problems that a sociological approach has with such exploration is the way in which the 'interiorities' can threaten to be too parochial, too cut off from the wider concerns of globalization, environmental change, poverty, the changing forms of capitalism and post-colonialism.[2] When, for example, the operations of the family could be analysed to reveal the clear relationship between the gendered domestic division of labour and the reproduction of cap-italism (Barrett and McIntosh, 1982) it was seen as justified to draw attention to the private sphere and the local because doing so explained part of the bigger picture. But the decline in these grand theories appears to have robbed such studies of this justification. Theories of individualization (discussed in chapter 1) have to some extent revitalized an interest in what is now referred to as intimacy rather than the private sphere, so it would seem that sociological interest waxes and wanes depending on whether direct theoretical links can be made with a wider social condition and intimate or personal life. Thus sociology was interested in families when they were theorized to reproduce capitalism, while the later interest in personal relationships has become justified through the light thrown on global processes of individualization. This, I suggest, is soci-ology's structuralist legacy, which has created a hierarchy of (moral) significance within the discipline. This hierarchy has not prevented other interests or ways of doing sociology from emerging but, when

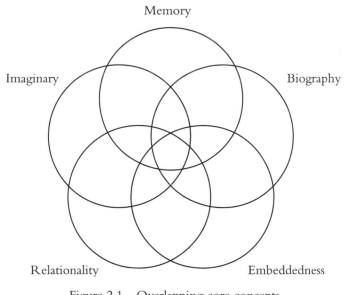

Memory

Imaginary

Biography

Relationality

Embeddedness

Figure 2.1   Overlapping core concepts

combined with the familiarity of everyday family living, discussions of interiority tend to come across as rather marginal.

In order to explore interiority and, ultimately, to show how it is not a separate sphere that needs to be connected with an outer sphere, it is necessary to consider a range of concepts and ideas and to show how they may be linked to form a new chain of thought. Each of these areas merits a book-length exegesis and indeed most of them have generated this level of attention. But my purpose here is not to give each concept a separate in-depth discussion but to sketch out the field and to relate each to my site of interest, namely personal life. The concepts outlined in this chapter are explored more fully as the book unfolds, namely memory, biography, embeddedness, relationality and the imaginary. They can be seen as overlapping areas of theoretical exploration, as represented in figure 2.1. They are not entirely separate from one another and are mutually invested in each other. Nor do these named concepts necessarily constitute a complete list or set of issues but, taken together, they are intended to complement and build on Morgan's approach which focuses on practices. Although these conceptual fields may include what are commonly regarded as practices ('doing'), I want to emphasize the importance of thinking and imagining family and relationships. The duality of thinking and doing is itself somewhat problematic (Mason, 1996; Griffiths, 1995; Turner, 1984) but, before showing how entwined the thinking and doing are in practice, I introduce the two activities here to lead to a different way of understanding the experiences of living personal life.

Memory

As Barbara Misztal has stated: '[I]f the role of sociology is to investigate the different ways in which humans give meaning to the world [. . .], and if memory is crucial to our ability to make sense of our present circumstances, researching collective memory should be one of its most important tasks' (2003: 1). Her book makes a prolonged and extremely valuable case for sociology to (re)turn its attention to the social significance of memory. Her attentiveness to this area is matched by a growing interest in other social and cultural sciences and a rush of conferences and publications in the field (Radstone, 2000: 1). Memory has become a popular site of investigation: it has the capacity to bring disciplines together, to blur disciplinary boundaries and – for sociology at least – to impose an insistence that the past still matters. However, as Misztal states, memory is far from being only the ability to recall past events or acquired knowledge. While the definition of memory as the capacity to remember requires an individual to do the remembering, it is clearly impossible for anybody to remember everything. This means that it requires processes of selection which in turn require the means by which to select. These means are acquired interactively or socially, and the development of memory thus becomes laden with values that guide our selection. So while it is possible to discuss social or collective memory (the common focus of sociology, found in forms of commemoration, museums and local history societies), even individual memory is social. Individual memory is formed and shaped by others around us, especially through the process of language development since to have memories requires, in the main, an articulation of events or experiences so that they can be captured in memory.

But, as Misztal also points out, what we remember is closely associated with emotions. Put simply, we remember very happy or very sad occasions best because we have invested emotional capital in them. Moreover, when the same emotions are triggered by some new event, memories of former events can in turn intensify our feelings. So, on the one hand memories are embedded with emotions, so feelings influence what we recall (and what we forget). But, on the other hand, individual memory is also profoundly social because it relies on context to be meaningful and on communication to become a memory. The significance of this attention to memory for our understanding of family and relationships is several-fold. First, our earliest and possibly most intense memories are formed in the context of families – with parents or caring adults, perhaps also with one or more siblings. These social relationships are also the context for some of the most passionate emotional experiences we may have, whether feelings of love or rejection/hate, spite/jealousy, warmth/security or fear and so on (Mauthner, 2005). The fact that these memories are likely to be attached to early emotions begins to explain why getting involved in the history of one's own family – discovering old photographs, diaries and correspondence and so on – can be utterly compelling. Whether the feelings evoked are good or bad, they hold a peculiarly alluring and nostalgic significance. The emotional reaction to these memories when constructed in the present shifts 'the family' into a special place in our internal calibrations of personal significance. So although recall is often a largely conscious process, what is recalled may come with layers of meaning and significance, of emotions and desires, which go beyond the simply rational or conscious.[3] There is therefore a circular process in which families occupy a special place in the 'laying down' of strong memories, but the feelings generated by remembering one's childhood in a family can create anew the sense that these memories feed into a possibly unwarranted 'intuition' about the importance of one's family. Thus the more work we do in Western cultures on family memories and tracing lines of heritage, the more we contribute to the increasingly iconic status of families in our cultural imaginary.

Second, families provide the context in which we learn what to remember and what to forget. Hence photographs and later also videos are taken of 'special moments' as memory aids; certain events are rehearsed over and over again, often to the point when one does not know if one's memory is one's own or acquired from others through the constant retelling. Misztal (2003: 15) points out that families are mnemonic communities, in other words the family influences how much we remember of the past (especially the past that occurred before our arrival); that community shapes what and how we remember, and through creating shared memories gives family members a sense of shared history and identity (see also Carsten, 2000). These shared memories also create familiarity, which means that even people (ancestors) whom we have never met can feel part of the family and even our parents' own childhoods may be made to feel part of our own experience. Hence the creation of memories, especially shared memories, creates strong bonds, even if these bonds ultimately feel restrictive and negative for some.

Finally we need to grasp the chameleon nature of memory. Talja Blokland (2005) argues that memory has magical qualities in that it changes shape and colour depending on who is recalling events or processes, when they are doing so, and arguably why they are doing so. She stresses that memory is linked to the present; this insight – although not new – is particularly important for understanding families. It seems that there are particular moments when we are likely to remember our childhoods or our family history. These may be done collectively at times of a particular event, whether part of an annual ritual (e.g. Christmas) or part of a cultural celebration (e.g. weddings) or they may be more individual acts, such as when a parent dies, when children are born, or through the process of ageing. Whether these acts of remembering are collective or individual they take on different complexions according to the demands of the present moment. So, for example, as one ages memories may 'soften' so that recollections of parental punishment may shift from being interpreted as cruel to become evidence of 'tough love'; or memories of fear become retold as 'adventures'; or memory stories told to children may take on moral endings that are pure embell-ishment. Memories can change to suit an audience or to fit a newly crafted identity. Hence memories of initial sexual encounters might shift from delicate ones of inexperience to harsh ones of comic ineptitude. In the context of divorce or separation it is often noted how what might be called one's 'memory box' – to use Margaret Forster's title of 2000 to denote any collection of memories and memorabilia – can be switched from one containing precious times and moments to one completely overflowing with remembered slights, abuse, neglect and diminishment. Memory therefore works in unstable ways, notwithstanding that it almost always appears to have the status of the most authentic and most signifying act of identity creation.

Biography

In a similar vein to the growth of sociological interest in memory, there has been a development in the significance of biographical methods for enlarging and deepening the sociological imagination. Michael Rustin (2000) has written on the 'biographical turn' in sociology, which he identifies as arising from the 'cultural turn' and its increased interest in literature, art and narrative as well as the more obvious areas of the media and film. But Rustin argues that the biographical turn is more fragile than the cultural because it appears to be antithetical to the original aims and purposes of sociology. Incorporating biography into sociology requires two moves, first to give a recognized status to the explanatory value of the case-study approach, and second to allow a sense of much greater agency for the individual (even to influence culture and structure) than is normally tolerated. The individual has not been a unit of analysis for sociology, not only because the discipline has almost always seen the individual as responding to, or being the victim of, larger social forces, but also because the individual has been defined as belonging to the terrain of such disciplines as psychology and psycho-analysis. For sociology to start to be interested in individuals requires the overcoming of a long-standing boundary dispute.

Although I would argue that sociology has moved much further to embrace qualitative methodologies (and accompanying

epistemologies and ontologies) than Rustin appears to acknowledge, he is quite accurate in his analysis of the way in which parts
of the discipline find it hard to grasp the sociological significance
of the individual life story. Yet as social and cultural historians have
shown, a few lives – purposively selected – can capture a complex
picture of social change and connections with networks of kin;
these stories, whether they feature employment, migration or other
large-scale movements, can be located in an understanding of local
and dominant economic systems at the same time as they are situated in time. But perhaps more significantly, they can offer the
experience of living through certain times; they can deal with the
meanings that individuals attribute to events and relationships and
they can explain, to a degree, motivations, desires and aspirations.
These methodologies provide what have become known as 'thick
descriptions' (Geertz, 1973; Mason, 2002) because they create both
deep and dense understandings of processes and interactions. Yet,
as Rustin argues, as long as these descriptions relate to a sociological
viewpoint which is more concerned with the discovery of shared
processes and social context than with individuals *per se*, then
what emerges has a broader significance than the life of one or two
individuals.

The biographical turn has particular salience for understanding
family relationships. Most important is the ability to grasp movement through time (e.g. recognizing distinguishing features between
one decade and the next) but also movement through the life course
(e.g. the change that takes place between the ages of twenty and
thirty). It can also capture the different experiences of different
members of families or kin groups rather than treating them as a
homogeneous whole with one world view and one shared set of
experiences. Of course there are disadvantages too. Biography relies
on memory and, as discussed above, memory can be 'magical' and a
reliance on memory can produce an understanding of the past that
is filtered through the present. But biographical methods deploy
what might be visualized as little anchors for memory and which
give reference points to stories. These may be photographs, objects,
diaries or other documentary accounts. Thus, at least where studies
of family life are concerned, materiality becomes an important
feature of the biographical method. Not only do material objects

elicit memories and stories, but they also 'speak' themselves of particular decades, of specific tastes, or even of impoverishment or affluence. Anthropologists such as Daniel Miller (1998, 2001) and Tony Chapman and Jenny Hockey (1999) have emphasized the importance of homes, both objects and forms within homes and the (changing) meanings of a home. But they also point to the ways in which the social organization of the home gives insights into social relationships. Thus, at a most superficial level, separate bedrooms may be indicative of couple relationships; the frills on Austrian blinds or girly images from the Pirelli Calendar might speak of gender relationships; and untouched 'parlours' may speak of social relationships with others outside the home or even of class expectations. Anat Hecht argues that furniture, décor and ornaments 'are more than mere "things", they are a collection of appropriated materials, invested with meaning and memory, a material testament of who we are, where we have been, and perhaps even where we are heading' (2001: 123). Given the value of this anthropological work on homes and the link between homes and biography and memory, it is surprising that so few sociologists have extended their interest in intimacy and personal relationships to the places where these relationships occur (but see Morgan, 1996; Silva, 1999).

Embeddedness

The concept of embeddedness is not of the same order as the concepts discussed so far. It is more of an emergent and descriptive theme than a methodology or field of enquiry. However, it is particularly important in its capacity as the counterweight to concepts of individualism, liquidity or even the older 'anomie'. I discuss contemporary theories of relationships above (chapter 1), and the emphasis on the fragile bonds of couple relationships and the idea that people now invest differently in relationships making them more likely to be terminated than to endure. I also discuss the idea of the 'traditional' family or marriage which assumed that commitment was based on stable foundations, and that relationships were both durable and infused with desirable values. While acknowledging that these analyses capture some of the qualities of contemporary family life and relationships, I wish to argue that qualitative empirical research has provided contrasting accounts which suggest that it is problematic to confuse families with, or reduce them to, dyadic couple relationships and that even couple relationships may not be as liquid, contingent or 'pure' as is often depicted.

One of the main 'discoveries' of empirical research since the mid-1990s, focusing on what families 'do' rather than what families look like or what they are for, is that people have kin. I discuss kinship further in the next section but here I want to draw attention to the rediscovery that vertical kinship matters (children, parents, grandparents and even ancestors) (Finch and Mason, 2000; Mitchell and Green, 2002; Smart, 2005a; Brannen, Moss and Mooney, 2004). Longitudinal research has devised methodological tools to capture generational and cohort change; the previous reliance on snapshots of family life tended to prioritize parents living together with their children as if they were a bounded unit. In particular the work of Vern Bengtson et al. (2002) has offered a very different interpretation of how families change: family members were interviewed over three decades (starting in 1970), with four generations included in the study. Through repeat interviewing (including qualitative interviews) this study allowed the researchers to ask different generations of family members the same questions at the same stage of the life course. Thus, for example, they could ask young people what their relationship with their grandparents was like, and they could compare this with what the same young person's parents had said about their own grandparents when they had been the same age as their children. This allowed the researchers to get a grip on change (or continuity) while also revealing that wider kin remained very important to contemporary youth (in the USA). They deployed the concept of 'linked lives' as a way of describing chains of relationships across generations. They argued that individual life trajectories are meaningful in the context of the other lives with whom they are linked. So although these were 'individuals', their lives should not be seen in isolation from those other lives which ran in parallel, crossed and interfered with that of the subject. But more than this, they argued that it was important to theorize how each individual life was also embedded in a web of relationships which included people who had gone before (and who could also be dead). Previous generations left their mark, so to speak, on present generations. Elements of the past were carried forward and helped to form the apparently unique individual who was in fact taking forward part of the past.

This conceptualization of families across time captures an element of family life which can either offer ontological security or be experienced as psychologically and emotionally suffocating, and this is the issue of how hard it is to be free of one's family and kin. Where lives have become interwoven and embedded (at a material, emotional and metaphorical level) it becomes impossible for relationships to simply end. We now appreciate that family relationships do not necessarily end with death and that people have symbolic means, and even practices, which sustain elements of love and closeness (or even hate and bitterness). We also know that even those who have fled their families (e.g. after coming out or to marry the 'wrong' person) engage in imaginary conversations, or carry emotions about their families, in perpetuity. These relationships are very 'sticky'; it is hard to shake free from them at an emotional level and their existence can continue to influence our practices and not just our thoughts.

Embeddedness is therefore neither a good nor a bad quality in family or other relationships; it can take either form – and indeed many in between. But as a concept it seeks to reflect the tenacity of these bonds and links, sometimes even to the extent that family members and close kin or friends can feel as if they were part of one. This 'being a part of one' can manifest itself in several ways, whether close physical resemblance, or in a shared aptitude, aesthetic taste or sense of values. Thus it can be hard to forget a mother or father if each day one looks more and more like her/him. It is equally hard to forget a divorced spouse if every day one's child looks or sounds more and more like him/her. Blood relationships in particular seem to be unique in possessing these haunting powers. I say more about this in the last section of this chapter, 'imaginary'. But here I wish to stress the materiality of these feelings and associations and hence the importance of always putting the individual in the context of their past, their webs of relationships, their possessions and their sense of location.

Relationality

The concept of relationality (also known as relationism) has emerged from the convergence of studies on kinship within both anthropology and sociology. In this section I outline the way in which this frame of reference has developed before discussing how it relates to my overall theme of the cultural turn in family research.

Janet Carsten has mapped meticulously the shift in anthropological thinking away from 'older' approaches to understanding kinship towards the 'new' kinship studies. Part of this shift has entailed the adoption of different terminology such that she argues that anthropology is now concerned with 'relatedness' rather than with formal structures of kinship (2004: 109). Relatedness, as a term, is a different way of expressing two main themes. The first is that individuals are constituted through their close kin ties; in other words, without both formative and on-going relationships we do not develop our own sense of personhood or even individuality. As Carsten acknowledges, this is not a new insight but one that keeps being submerged in the Western intellectual tradition with its emphasis on the bounded individual, one who may seek out relationships or connectedness but who can exist independently of others. Indeed, it is possible to see that in Western thinking the very idea of the individual is one who has forged himself by rejecting the influences of others and by denying his connectedness with others (Griffiths, 1995).[4] The second theme is that the kin to whom we relate in this process no longer need to be blood relatives. Although the new kinship in anthropology preserves the cultural and personal significance of blood ties (and the slightly more abstract notion of genetic ties), this approach gives equal importance to people who may not be strictly 'kin' at all, but who occupy the same place in emotional, cultural, locational and personal senses. This expands the range of significant others that anthropology or sociology can grasp as formative in the lives of ordinary people. Sociology's focus on couples and their children, for example, has ignored almost completely the importance of sibling relationships (Mauthner, 2005); equally in anthropology the focus on lineage and/or property has meant that the quality of relationships was long deemed barely worthy of comment. The concept of relatedness therefore takes as its starting point what matters to people and how their lives unfold in specific contexts and places. Jeanette Edwards has captured this in her study of relatedness (through an investigation of new reproductive technologies) in the small town of Bacup in Lancashire. In reporting how such ordinary people see kinship, Edwards states:

> On the one hand, affective ties between kin develop, it is said, through the experiences of growing up, and growing up in a particular place, at a particular time, with particular people *moulds* a specific character. On the other hand, the facts of human conception (knowledge of the origins of gametes and the fixed genetic inheritances with which a person is born) are integral to the formation of a new individual. To be born and to be bred is to be constituted of relationships that are both affective ties *and* abstract connections between persons. (2000: 29; emphasis in original)

Edwards has gone so far as to invent the concept of 'born and bred' kinship; the phrase 'born and bred' has many resonances in English usage, though here it is intended to capture the combination of genetic/blood relationship with place, context and moment. Through understanding 'born and bred' kinship it becomes possible to 'think about' how people relate to one another on several different conceptual planes at the same time.

At the same time as anthropology was going through this epistemological break, Janet Finch and Jennifer Mason were developing different ways of thinking about families and kin in sociology. In 1989, when Finch published *Family Obligations and Social Change*, 'kin' was not a term that was often used in sociology; 'the family' had been reduced to refer to the nuclear family with a presumption of co-residence in one household. This book was followed by further work on family obligations and negotiations (Finch and Mason, 1993, 2000) in which the conceptualization of kin and kinship became increasingly important and sophisticated. Initially 'kin' appears to have been used as a synonym for 'relatives', and thus served a largely descriptive function. But over time it became the conceptual tool through which Finch and Mason fashioned new ways of understanding complex relationships among people who defined themselves as related. Finch's initial concerns were to challenge the rigid and unrealistic model of family life (structure) held in the minds of policy makers and to problematize the notion of duty between kin. On the one hand she argued that kinship (in England) is more fluid and dynamic than the usual static model of fixed relationships allows. On the other she argued that family obligations and exchanges were based on 'persons' not 'positions'. By this she meant that a sense of duty might or might not develop between relations simply because one was a grandmother or a cousin. However, feelings of affection or obligation towards certain individuals would usually result from a history of interaction and reciprocity. These ideas came to coalesce into a kind of sociological version of anthropology's 'new kinship'. As Finch and Mason put it:

> First, we think that kinship operates at, or is to be found at, the level of *negotiated relationships* more than structures or systems. [. . .] Essentially, this is why we wish to jettison both the idea of kinship as a structure and the concept of individualism in favour of one of *relationism*. Second, we want to suggest that kinship is constituted in *relational practices*, with the privilege that this concept gives to actors' reasoning, actions and experiences. (2001: 164; emphases in original)

Relationality is a most important concept because it transcends the limitations of that of kinship, which no matter how redefined can still carry outmoded connotations. The word itself clearly acknowledges that people *relate* to others who are not necessarily kin by 'blood' or marriage, thus allowing for considerable flexibility in approach, including such ideas as 'families of choice' (Weston, 1991). But perhaps even more significantly, it captures a way of thinking and also expresses motivations that ordinary people may have. For example Mason (2004), in exploring the ways in which people explain decisions to move home, found that their relationships with others (predominantly but not exclusively family) played a substantial role in their reasoning. The term 'relationism' conjures up the image of people existing within intentional, thoughtful networks which they actively sustain, maintain or allow to atrophy.

Indeed, the combination of relationism with the term 'practices' (derived from Morgan, 1996) also emphasizes the active nature of relating and reduces the idea that relationships are simply given (and hence unchanging) through one's position in a family genealogy. In her paper on residential histories, Mason (2004) also points out that relational thinking does not have to imply affectionate bonds or a desire to be near one's relatives or wider kin. On the contrary, it might drive a person from one part of the country to another, precisely to be removed from certain people, expectations or influences. So the concept does not necessarily denote a warm, loving and consensual web of relationships. Indeed, from her earliest work in 1989 Finch has been aware of the antipathies of kinship and that feelings for and about relatives are not always positive.[5]

Relationality is then a mode of thinking which not only influences decisions and choices, but also forms a context for the unfolding of everyday life. But it is not just a state of mind, it requires action. This brings me back to my earlier point about the distinction between mind (thought) and body (practices). Although it is important to stress the significance of 'thought' as a means of countering the rather materialist or functionalist focus of many previous sociological theorizations of family life, it is equally important to recognize that thought and action permeate one another. Family practices do not occur without thought, however ritualized some of them may become. This leads me to the final section of this chapter, the realm of the imaginary.

Imaginary

The ways in which relationships exist (indeed have a life) in one's imagination and thoughts can be expressed in terms of the 'imaginary', which is not limited to individual or personal imaginings but also connects with the social and cultural level. This means that our personal musings, desires, thoughts and emotions about and around relationships are not entirely individual because they are formed in social and historical contexts; many others have much the same feelings as our own. Thus a person who has been adopted in infancy may develop a strong desire to find his or her birth mother; but this is not a unique feeling, no matter how personal and even private it may feel to the individual. Indeed, so many adopted people have expressed this feeling that it is now quite socially acceptable to do so (although it hardly ever happened before the 1980s and 1990s). The social context may not determine what a person feels about relationships, but it would seem that there is a complex interplay between social mores and at least some of the personal feelings we may experience. Gillis (2004), for example, has traced the ways in which English and American cultures have responded to death and has shown that, since Victorian times, both practices and acceptable emotions have changed in terms of what is deemed to be appropriate, whether applied to length of mourning or types of ritual, clothing or other forms of display. We cannot necessarily assume that everyone's sensibilities marched in unison with these changing mores, but the point is that personal feelings are linked with social transformations and have social consequences and meanings.

There is also a cultural level to the imaginary of family life and relationships. This is where specific ideals of families or assumptions about family life are reproduced. Examples abound in magazines (usually for women), on television, in the popular press and in lightweight fiction. Nostalgic and usually idealized forms of family are recollected in evocations of 'proper' family life in bygone eras. The idea that there was a time when families stayed together, when children could be children until the proper time, when grandparents were cared for and when mothers remained at home (happily) to do their proper duty has become a positive mantra of yearning (Gillis, 1996). But this imaginary realm of family can also take the form of expectations for the future (the big wedding where parent and child will be reconciled, or the prospect of the birth of a child to consolidate a relationship). Furthermore, it can haunt the present (for example at annual festivals, whether religious or commercial, when everyone else's family appears 'normal' and happy when one's own is not). As Gillis has expressed it:

> Often fragmented and impermanent, [the families we live with] are much less reliable than the imagined families we live by. The latter are

never allowed to let us down. Constituted through myth, ritual, and image, they must be forever nurturing and protective, and we will go to any lengths to ensure that they are so, even if it means mystifying the realities of family life. (1996: xv)

Gillis refers to two realms of family life: the families we live 'with' and those we live 'by'. The latter inhabit our imaginations but they constantly impinge upon our actual routine practices; they are therefore not confined to daydreams or reminiscences. He suggests that we work towards the ideal by planning family holidays, by organizing family gatherings, by filling family albums with smiling photos, and by such conventions as never speaking ill of the dead. This realm of the imaginary is therefore to be construed as a family practice as much as a set of thoughts or wishes. Gillis argues that we actively engage in sustaining the cultural imaginary of family life.

This leads full circle back to the starting point of this chapter, with its discussions of memory and biography. Through the work of Gillis we can see that rituals of remembering or of narrating stories about family are constitutive of a cultural level of meaning about families and relationships. An iterative process can be envisaged in which personal feelings and emotions become sedimented into ways of responding and ways of knowing within families; the cultural and historical contexts in which these occur, however, imply (rather than dictate) the shape and form that they might take. This means that families can be experienced as unique, while also reflecting social conventions and reproducing commonplace rituals and practices. By including an analysis of the imaginary realm in terms of family, we can connect not only with what appears to matter to people but with everyday concerns at a remarkably broad cultural and social level of significance. The idea that the interiority of family life is unimportant unless it can be linked to a meta-theory such as the reproduction of capitalist relations is therefore challenged. This way of thinking does not necessarily support one particular account or theory, rather it offers conceptual links between spheres such that it becomes possible to trace 'the workings' of things. This approach is akin to the methodological thinking of Foucault or Bourdieu, in which theorization is depicted not as a goal to be achieved, but as a toolbox full of insights that can be put together creatively to form flexible modes of analysis. It thus becomes possible to grasp different dimensions both severally and together.

★   ★   ★

This chapter has sought to explore the ways in which we can bring together ideas that are being developed in the field of relationship research and, in so doing, to create a new approach which offers possible ways ahead for future empirical research. The fields of memory, biography, embeddedness, relationality and the imaginary are not entirely discrete, they overlap and merge and it is easy to slide from one into another. But this is not a problem because the areas of personal life they seek to capture are not discrete or bounded either. It may be impossible to explore all of these areas simultaneously, but the point is that seen as a whole they can encourage a shift in the level of complexity at which it is possible to work when dealing with personal life and relationships. Thus depth and contours can be captured through attentiveness to memory (both cultural and personal), and the sedimented layers of the past that shape or influence the present can thus be appreciated. Implicit within this approach is an encouragement always to seek for meaning, even in the apparently mundane and everyday, and even invested in inanimate objects. This chapter's implicit acknowledgement of the salient role that families play in the creation of memory and in the importance of family traditions and histories is developed in subsequent chapters, but it is important here to understand that this is not a way of uncritically reinstating 'the family' in the lexicon of sociology. Rather it is part of the project of understanding the iconic nature of 'the family' which has such an important cultural impact in post-industrial societies. I now go on to try to draw in some of these threads, to explore the possibility of developing different ways of knowing and analysing personal life.

3

Emotions, Love and the Problem of Commitment

Sociological understandings of intimate relationships and family life are from time to time rebuked for paying insufficient attention to the ways in which such relationships are saturated with emotions, feelings and affect (Jackson, 1993; Duncombe and Marsden, 1993; Hochschild, 1975). Indeed, the whole of the discipline has been the focus of similar criticism. But such claims are equally often disputed; Chris Shilling (2002), for example, provides a robust defence of the founding fathers of sociology who, he argues, took the emotions very seriously in their grand theorizing. He suggests that it is an inattentiveness to their work that has created the impression that the realm of the emotions has been absent from the sociological imagination. Moreover contemporary social theorists have recently turned their attention to the emotions in a deliberate attempt to foreground their importance in all aspects of social and economic life (Barbalet, 1998; Barbalet, ed., 2002; Burkitt, 1997, 2002; Lupton, 1998; Sayer, 2005). And it is also the case that feminist work within sociology (and work more widely) has been attentive to emotions, particularly in the context of heterosexual relationships as considered by authors ranging from Simone de Beauvoir (1972, French orig. 1949) to Wendy Langford (1999). This criticism of sociology therefore seems misplaced because it is possible to find evidence of discussions of emotions (even love) in a number of fields. But there remains a doubt about the real impact of this work. As Shilling acknowledges:

> If the subject of emotions is now recognized as crucial to a comprehensive understanding of key sociological questions, it would appear that the sub-discipline has come of age. Paradoxically, however, the relationship between the sociology of emotions and mainstream sociology remains relatively cool. (2002: 11)

This coolness is perhaps unsurprising because there remains a fairly firm assumption that emotions are the domain of psychology or, even more worryingly, of evolutionary biology and that to trespass on these areas means that one is necessarily abandoning a sociological approach.

In this chapter I therefore consider sociological work on emotions, some of which is overcoming the 'coolness' that Shilling refers to; this provides a context for the ensuing discussion of love and commitment. If sociology has been cool towards emotions in general, then its approach to love can only be described as frosty. This view has given rise to a preference for studying and analysing issues that may be 'near to' love (e.g. care, commitment, sex, marriage, romance) but which can not really be taken as love by another name. Of these issues 'near to' love, it has been that of commitment which has come to dominate sociological interest and I therefore examine how this focus turns attention away from the importance of affections in everyday life towards more readily calibrated notions of duty, obligation and even contract. The chapter ends with an exploration of these questions through the ideas generated by a qualitative interview-based study that a research team (including Jennifer Mason, Beccy Shipman and me) carried out on gay and lesbian marriage.[1] In this way I aim to introduce the ways in which people themselves locate the significance of both love and commitment in their relationships.

Understanding emotions sociologically

Deborah Lupton (1998) has produced one of the most engaging studies of the field among the increasing numbers of volumes about emotion. Initially she identifies types of sociological approach to emotions, thus providing a useful typology for mapping the field. She puts these under two broad umbrellas – the emotions as inherent and the emotions as socio-cultural constructs. Under the first she places those who interpret emotions as genetic or given and within which emotions are seen to be reflexes and thus fairly universal in human kind. Importantly she identifies in this strand those who see emotions as 'animalistic' and in need of civilization and restraint which in turn reflects the Enlightenment idea that logic and reason are superior to base emotion. It is also linked to the pervasive notion that women (being supposedly less evolved than men) have more emotions (or their emotions are nearer the surface), while men have achieved the ideal of reason and objectivity. Lupton's second type, namely socio-cultural constructions of emotion, are considerably more developed. To put it briefly, she refers to four approaches, the structuralist, the phenomenological, the post-structuralist and the psycho-dynamic approaches. She sees the structuralist approach as dominant and points to the work of the founding fathers Marx, Weber and Durkheim (viz. Shilling above) as well as Elias (2000, orig. 1939) and Hochschild (2003). What these theorists have in common is that they focus on the ways in which different social systems produce different emotions and how emotions can be harnessed, manipulated or directed to meet the needs of the system. As Lupton mentions, the strength of this approach is that it acknowledges the cultural plasticity of emotions and also replaces the essentialist notion of 'naturalness' with the sociological concept of power and/or social context. In this approach emotions are given a history rather than a timeless quality.

The phenomenological approach draws on the philosophy of Jean-Paul Sartre (1993, French orig. 1939) and Maurice Merleau-Ponty (1962, French orig. 1945), which was later developed sociologically by Norman Denzin (1984). The key element of this approach is the focus on the individual's relationship with the social world and the way in which already acculturated individuals interpret both their milieu and their feelings. In this way – in contradistinction to the structuralist approach – the person becomes the key interpreter of emotions which are, in turn, intersubjectively produced. While those who understand emotions to be genetic or inherent take them to be internally generated, phenomenologists see them as generated through interactions with others. Moreover, the individual is engaged in cognitive interpretation of his or her feelings and this process is understood to be part of the formation of the self. It is important to realize that while a person's sense of self is seen to develop through the routine of emotional practice and reflection, the phenomenological approach involves believing that this process creates a 'true' self. This is a constructed self rather than a given or natural self, but it is nonetheless taken to be an authentic self. Ultimately it becomes possible for a person to pretend to have certain emotions which are not 'true'; emotions can therefore become alienated in a way that comes close to that of Hochschild's focus on the capitalist appropriation and distortion of, in particular, women's emotions.

The post-structuralist approach, according to Lupton, has focused predominantly on the discursive construction of emotions; this means not only noting what is said about emotions or the deployment of particular 'emotion' scripts, but also that the subject is produced in the articulation of the discourse. Hence women, rather than men, are discursively constructed as emotional and this stands in opposition to those who assume that women are naturally more expressive of their emotions than men are. The focus on discourse has allowed for much exploration of cultural productions of emotions (e.g. the romantic novel, women's magazines) and has also given rise to a sociological approach to emotions which seeks only to explore these cultural manifestations and how people engage with them, rather than looking 'inwards' towards the self. As Stevi Jackson (1993) has argued, sociologists can access emotions only through what people say about them so that the project is inevitably focused on the discursive.

The psycho-dynamic approach, by contrast, aims to go beyond what is said about emotions to some deeper level. It does not assume that emotions are represented (to the self and to others) through cognition or rational reflection, but sees emotions as relating to the extra-rational and/or the unconscious. It takes relationality or interaction as a crucial element in understanding emotions (e.g. the infant's early interactions with her or his mother) but the generation of feelings and the significance of these feelings is played out in the unconscious rather than in the language-based realm of consciousness (not least because the foundations of emotions are pre-linguistic). So, for the psycho-dynamic approach, there is always a foundation of emotions and emotional reaction and understanding which is laid before language and this remains in place – albeit hidden. This means that, from this perspective at least, sociology alone cannot access a full understanding of emotions because, without applying some variant of psychoanalysis, it cannot account for the unconscious wherein lies the perpetual source of emotions.

Having mapped the field in this way, Lupton proceeds to outline her own position, taking elements from each of the socio-cultural constructionist approaches above, save perhaps the psycho-dynamic, which she sees as important but as something that 'requires incorporation' into the general approach – but presumably by someone else. She states:

> I am interested in the lived experience and social relational dimension of emotions, including the role played by such factors as gender and power relations in emotional experience. However, I avoid the notion of the 'true' emotional self that tends to be articulated in structuralist and phenomenological accounts for a poststructuralist perspective on subjectivity that sees it as dynamic and shifting, and as constituted, rather than distorted or manipulated by, sociocultural processes. I acknowledge that discourse plays a vital role in constructing and shaping emotional experience. (Lupton, 1998: 38)

To this I would add two further dimensions, or perhaps it is more accurate to call them 'inflections' because they are potentially incorporated into the mapped socio-cultural constructionist approaches already. These would be the ideas of 'the magical' as highlighted by Nick Crossley (1998) and originally derived from Sartre, and relationality as emphasized by Ian Burkitt (1997). For the former, Crossley argues that the concept of the magical 'allows us to grasp emotions as specific ("enchanted") ways of being-in-the-world, open for analysis, and to avoid the tendency to view them negatively as failures in instrumental reasoning' (1998: 29). My take on this is to share with Crossley the idea that not everything is rational or instrumental and to suggest further that it is the realm of the emotions that makes everyday living valuable and worthwhile rather than just sensible and inevitable. The idea that emotional experiences can be somewhat transcendental and intangible is important if sociology is to depict a more complex image of people's lives. Lupton is close to this too when she argues that the 'very mutability, ephemerality and intangible nature of "the emotions", as well as their inextricable interlinking with and emergence from constantly changing social, cultural and historical contexts, means that they are not amenable to precise categorization' (1998: 5).

The concept of relationality is discussed in chapter 2 but it is helpful to restate it here because of the importance of recognizing that emotions do not spring from the self-contained individual but are produced and given meaning in a socio-cultural (or self-reflexive) context. It is in part through emotions that we communicate and emotions give meaning to our communications and, as Burkitt emphasizes, in part quoting Kenneth Gergen (1994), 'emotions do not have an impact on social life; they constitute social life itself' (1997: 41). I take from this the imperative that we cannot grasp how people behave in relation to one another unless we are attentive to emotions and, even if one does not go as far as Gergen, his insistence that we cannot understand what things mean to people without an appreciation of the emotions is well taken.

All these contributions to the sociological discussion of emotions point to the absolute centrality of emotions to social and personal life and yet this returns us to Shilling's remark at the start of this chapter, namely that the relationship between mainstream sociology and this subfield remains cool. In other words not everyone is convinced. Perhaps it is simply more apt to recognize that there are theoretical and methodological difficulties involved in bringing emotions into the discipline (just as it was difficult to bring feminist approaches into an understanding of gender relations; or Foucaultian conceptualizations of power into a dominant Marxist paradigm; or relational conceptualizations of 'the family' into a predominantly functionalist arena). These difficulties seem even more magnified when one turns specifically to the emotions of love and affection which carry the 'stigma' of association with women's magazines or frivolous trivia. The seriousness of sociology as a discipline seems to become compromised if it gets too close to the taken-for-granted stuff of everyday life.

Taking love seriously

When looking at love analytically there is a tendency to divide it into discrete categories such as maternal love, companionate love, romantic love, sexual love, as if these are distinct types of affection to be found pre-packaged on a supermarket shelf, ready with their own sets of feelings and expectations about etiquette or decorum. Yet the boundaries between these 'types' are so fluid that it begins to seem that the distinctions are more an obstacle to understanding than a help. It is not that love does not have many different complexions, but if we see it both as a complex and as relational (and hence something that one 'does' and 'feels' with others, rather than a pre-existing type of emotion that one 'has'), then it is the context which gives specific meaning to the emotion. It would be naïve to imply that young people do not have expectations about certain emotions, and love in particular is subject to extensive discursive exploration in novels, media and popular self-help manuals. Hence in Western cultures most people expect to 'fall in love' at some stage, wonder whether romantic love will turn into companionate love and/or whether maternal love will be different from sexual love. But these expectations may not match experience; why else for example is so much advice available for those who seek reassurance about whether they *really* love another person? Why too do there seem to be so many mismatches between the expectations of heterosexual couples about what being in a loving relationship means (Mansfield and Collard, 1988)?

We also know that the complex relationship called love changes across the life course so that the love one might experience in relation to one's parents as a child may become a rather differently nuanced set of emotions once we are adults, even if it is still called love. Moreover, the acceptable range, scope and content of feelings held to constitute love may change over centuries or even decades (Elias, 2000). It may be in the West that a particular ideal of love,

namely romanticized love, has come to dominate expectations
through the medium of film, romantic novels, magazines and so on,
but this is really a question for research rather than assumption and
certainly the relationships between such representations and how
people actually 'do' love is still open to enquiry (Johnson, 2005).
The ever-variable complex of emotions referred to as love make it
difficult to grasp and yet it is apparent that love is closely related to
quality of life. As Jennifer Mason has argued (1996), there is a considerable experiential chasm between acts of care (e.g. preparing
food and helping another to eat) carried out with love and those
carried out without any feelings – even if the behaviour 'looks'
manifestly the same it 'feels' very different. Perhaps this is the
magical quality of the emotions: they can turn everyday acts into
interactions laden with meaning. If this is so, then it seems that the
way to incorporate emotions, particularly those associated with
love, into the sociological enterprise is to allow observations about
emotions into the methods and analysis of social research, rather
than documenting the visible behaviour or alighting solely on the
cognitive-rational kinds of explanation that dominate most interview transcripts. Before I pursue some of these ideas, however,
I now explore the ways in which sociological work has studiously
avoided love, either by treating it with disdain or by turning it into
something more 'fitting' to the sociological enterprise.

The disdainful approach

While this approach has been most marked in feminist work, others
have come to join the chorus of disdain, notably Beck and Beck-
Gernsheim (1995) and Bauman (2003). Feminist analysis of
heterosexual marriage, for example, identified love as part of
patriarchy's ideological armament through which women became
hooked into dependent relationships with men, entered into an
unfavourable legal contract (namely marriage) and ultimately ended
up with the care of the children. This idea of love as a means of
trapping women into marriage (or at the very least unequal heterosexual relationships) has long-standing feminist credentials from
Mary Wollstonecraft and Harriet Taylor (Mendus, 2000) to Simone

de Beauvoir (1972), via radical and socialist feminism of the 1970s and 1980s (e.g. Comer, 1974; Gavron, 1983; Jeffreys, 1985; Barry, 1979; Richardson, 1996) and on to Wendy Langford (1999) in the 1990s. Typically it has been argued that love itself, particularly in the form of romanticized love in fiction and film, offers women both transcendence and power (over men), as well as bringing happiness and fulfilment. Langford's argument goes further to suggest that heterosexual women turn themselves into people of a kind they think men want, for the sake of love. Thus love is not just economically or materially damaging, but damaging to the self. Underlying this argument is an assumption that love of the heterosexual other is a kind of 'false consciousness', against which women should guard themselves because in the context of manifest gender inequalities, heterosexual love can only reflect and re-create unequal power relations.

A lot of this feminist work has focused less on actual love relationships between men and women than on discursive representations of love, for example on Mills & Boon romances or the ways in which girls' magazines represent and prepare girls to 'fall in love' and accept the patriarchal nature of the love contract (McRobbie, 1991). As this work developed in cultural studies, however, questions were raised about whether women really did read romantic fiction quite so literally or whether these fictions were used as a means of escaping from everyday realities and drudgeries (Radway, 1984). The idea of romantic love as 'escape' rather than oppression came to mean that women ceased to be depicted as dupes who uncritically accept the patriarchal message. This view was then replaced with the idea that a fantasy life was a means of making the unequal power relationships between men and women tolerable. This, in turn, meant that women were seen as deflected from organizing to change their situation, and instead accommodate to it.

Empirical work on actual heterosexual love relationships (e.g. Mansfield and Collard, 1988) also reinforced the idea that women had very different expectations of marriage and relationships (and of love) than did men. Women often expected the romance of courtship to last into marriage, yet appeared to find that the intimacy could evaporate, in which case they felt emotionally abandoned. This work, combined with research which focused on issues of women's economic vulnerability, poverty in later life, violence in heterosexual relationships and the unequal burden of paid and unpaid work (e.g. Barrett and McIntosh, 1982; Dobash and Dobash, 1980; Wilson, 1977; Glendinning and Millar, 1987; Edwards, 1989), produced an intellectual climate hostile to the emotions generally, but to love in particular because it was seen as the ideological mask for the economic, sexual and physical exploitation of women by men. It was little wonder that there was no enthusiasm to approach emotions in a different way.

Love has also been taken up by theorists of individualization. Giddens (1992) has handled the topic relatively optimistically, identifying signs of increased democratization in heterosexual relationships, with women imposing their version of intimacy and love more forcefully upon men. He appears to argue that social and cultural equality influences the workings of love and that women's greater economic power, which allows them to leave unsatisfactory relationships, has given them greater influence over intimacies (see Jamieson, 1998, for a critique of this). But Giddens is somewhat exceptional in this genre. More typical is the view of love by Beck and Beck-Gernsheim (1995), which has been taken up in large part by Bauman and to some extent by Evans (2003). According to Beck and Beck-Gernsheim, love is a modern monster which makes us all resolutely individualistic; yet it fails to satisfy and thus easily turns into a destructive force.

> For individuals who have to invent or find their own social settings, love becomes the central pivot giving meaning to their lives. In this world where no one demands obedience or respect for old habits, love is exclusively in the first person singular, and so are truth, morality, salvation, transcendence and authenticity. [. . .] Growing out of itself and its own subjective views, it easily turns totalitarian; rejecting any outside authority, and agreeing to take over responsibility, to compromise and be fair only for emotional, spontaneous reasons. (1995: 171)

For these authors, love has become the secular religion of the individualized society. They argue that the forces of individualization make us crave love with intensity because we are so alone, yet precisely because we put so much store in love as our salvation, we are too often hugely disappointed, and once disappointed it seems we turn rather nasty. One more quotation captures the full disdain with which Beck and Beck-Gernsheim depict love:

> Love however should on no account be equated here with fulfilment. That is its glowing side, the physical thrill. Even [sex] does not mean fulfilment, or even require it. Achieving the goal often turns the sight of the flesh which seemed so delightful a moment ago into an alien white [sic] mass shorn of any appeal with the clothes so perfunctorily stripped off it. How easily having one's hopes fulfilled can turn into a chilly gaze! [. . .] now we are staring at each other with critical eyes, rather like meat inspectors, or even butchers who see the sausages where others see cattle and pigs. (1995: 12)

As with the earlier feminists, love is seen as a kind of ideology or religion which offers false hopes; the only real difference is that for Beck and Beck-Gernsheim both men and women are subject to its influence. It would also perhaps be true to say that these authors are convinced of both the shallowness and total social destructiveness of these emotions. In other words their disdain is on a grand scale. There is no subtlety here in their understanding of how emotions might 'work' or be created relationally, there is in a sense no redemption for love. While Giddens sees structural equality as giving rise to greater possibilities for a modern, positive and desirable kind of love and intimacy, for Beck and Beck-Gernsheim it is love that replaces the old evils of class inequalities with a new destructive gender war, a war that is destroying families and social values.

Bauman follows a similar theme, showing disgust with the shallowness of contemporary people who are concerned solely (or so he would have it) with relationships. He writes, like an Old Testament prophet of doom, castigating the inept fools who populate the modern landscape:

> This book's central characters are men and women, our [sic] contemporaries, despairing at being abandoned to their own wits and feeling easily disposable, yearning for the security of togetherness and for a helping hand to count on in a moment of trouble, and so desperate to 'relate'; yet wary of the state of 'being related' and particularly of being

related 'for good', not to mention forever [. . .] In our [*sic*] world of rampant 'individualization' relationships are a mixed blessing. They vacillate between sweet dream and a nightmare, and there is no telling when one turns into the other. (2003: viii)

As with Beck and Beck-Gernsheim, Bauman is fascinated by the flip side of (supposedly) casual love, which appears to be a kind of enduring hell. His portentous predictions about risks and anxieties and inevitable personal miseries are a thorough condemnation of the ways in which he sees his contemporaries as living.

In this context it is important to mention the contribution of Mary Evans (2003) who does, to some extent, share the more pessimistic vision of modern love expounded by the theorists of individualization. However, Evans distinguishes between the modern, commercialized variant of romanticized love, which she sees as over-hyped, unfulfilling and unreliable, and what she calls rational love. This is the kind of love she hopes will have a future because it entails care and attentiveness to others and it is part of a relationship that requires negotiation and commitment over time. She is critical of the search for a 'quick fix' kind of love, the delusion that once one has stumbled on love, it will be transformatory in its provision of happiness. So Evans does not reject love or emotions altogether but seeks to reunite care and commitment with love. The problem with this formulation, however, is that it presumes that these attributes have become disaggregated in everyday life. It also brings with it the idea that love is good (sociologically speaking) only if it entails work, self-sacrifice and some degree of compromise and endurance, otherwise known as commitment. These references to concepts like work and commitment lead to the next sociological strategy.

The translation approach

As outlined above, the sociological mode of dealing with love (or even affection) is to turn it into something that can be dealt with by existing conceptualizations. Typically this means turning love into 'work' (hence Hochschild's emotion work, 2003), or into care (for example labours of love), or finally into commitment (which can be measured by recourse to marriage and divorce rates: Morgan, 2000).

This translation strategy is set out clearly in Andrew Sayer's *The Moral Significance of Class* (2005). Sayer does not discuss love *per se* but, as his title suggests, he examines moral judgement and the moral significance of emotions, raising questions about why sociologists have avoided these dimensions in their accounts of the lived experiences of social class, notwithstanding the extent to which they are a part of everyday life. He basically argues that there are some things sociology will not address, either because they are presumed to be the focus of another discipline (e.g. philosophy or psychology) or because there seems to be no way of introducing aspects of everyday life without disrupting settled sociological frameworks. Put another way, some topics are simply outside sociology's field of vision, while those that might be disruptive are translated into more acceptable sociological concepts. Sayer takes the example of how sociology has tended to translate issues of morality into the idea of convention.[2] He suggests that if people explain/justify their behaviour in terms of morality, this must be acknowledged, not translated into something more comfortable. He argues:

> While sociologists are often content to reduce the moral to the conventional in their professional explanations of others' actions, they are unlikely to explain their own actions in this way, nor would they accept an appeal to 'what we do round here' as a justification of actions of others who behaved unethically towards them. This reduction is both inconsistent and demeaning. (2005: 46)

The idea that sociologists offer explanations for things that 'other' people do which they would not accept for themselves is a challenging one. It raises the question of whether sociologists regard themselves as the exceptions when they speak or write about the lives of ordinary people. To some extent Stevi Jackson seeks to address this in her article 'Even Sociologists Fall in Love' (1993), but the challenging title does not really fulfil its promise. Jackson does not ask the question of what it might mean for a sociological understanding of relationships and personal life that sociologists themselves experience and feel love. Rather she puts the case for studying love discursively, in other words to examine what has been written and is said about love. She thus tends to slip away from questions of feelings, appearing to move emotions into a kind of safe parallel universe in order to interrogate them. Her approach does not actually challenge how sociology thinks about love; rather she turns love into something that sociology can safely handle.

Sayer and Jackson in their different ways question whether the concept of commitment is a kind of sanitized, sociologically acceptable notion used instead of such emotionally charged (but much more everyday) words as love, which embraces a full gamut of associated feelings. So I now turn to a consideration of the significance of the concept of commitment.

About commitment/s

It is interesting to consider why sociological attention has come to focus on the issue of commitment. Public and political concern about high levels of divorce in the UK, USA and other industrialized societies has been voiced increasingly since the 1950s, so that the theme of decline in commitment or at least in the motivation to keep marriages intact has long been in circulation. More specifically governments have been concerned about the decline in marriage and the rise in co-habitation, reading into this the idea that people are avoiding commitment (Lewis, 2001; Popenoe, 1993). But although sociological interest often reflects and/or mirrors public and political concerns, it seems that commitment has also become part of the current interest in ideas of individualization and de-traditionalization. In other words, some analysts seem to hold that growing individualization brings with it not only a diminished capacity to love properly but also a diminishing capacity to commit to others or to relationships (see Duncan and Smith, 2006, and Jamieson, 1998 for critiques of this view). This issue is classically posed by Beck-Gernsheim: '[I]n sociological terms, how does the individualization drive of the last few decades enter ever more strongly into the area of the family, marriage and parenthood, effecting a lasting change in relations between the sexes and the generations?' (2002: 7–8). Similar questions can be found in a wide range of writings on family life.

So the focus on commitment is prompted from within sociology itself as well as from outside. The former is not hampered by a policy agenda, although the latter is often linked to a desire to develop policies which will re-create commitment, which will bolster marriage and which will encourage couples to 'work at' their relationships and be prepared for difficulties to come (Lewis, 2005; Eekelaar and Maclean, 2004; Jamieson et al., 2002). This political/policy agenda makes 'commitment' a difficult conceptual field for sociological enquiry because the term has become normative yet imbued with presumptions: that commitment is inherently good; if it is in decline, that is tragic; and that it is necessary to bolster commitment. In using the term one thus becomes tangled up with threads of politics, dogma, pro-family rhetoric, wildly incorrect historical generalizations, unsubstantiated generalizations and more besides.

These are good reasons to avoid the term but there may also be reasons to interrogate the concept itself and to consider the work it does in the sociological understanding of contemporary family life and relationships. And, following on from the discussions above about love, it seems important to think more about the relationship between commitment and love and explore how they overlap with one another. I propose therefore to draw on a study of same-sex commitment ceremonies and civil partnership in the UK that I conducted with Beccy Shipman and Jennifer Mason in 2004–6; this was based on fifty-four in-depth interviews (thirty-seven with couples and seventeen with individuals).[3] Because we started the study before civil partnership was made legally available in the UK in 2005, many of the people we interviewed had created their own forms of commitment ceremony and were going through the process notwithstanding the fact that they would achieve no legal rights or protections (Shipman and Smart, 2007). Thus it could be said that these were acts of 'pure' commitment because there were no or few social or legal benefits that followed the ceremony. However, all the couples wanted to have the legal rights that went with civil partnership and those we interviewed towards the close of our study made it clear that they would go through a second, formal process.

Arising from these interviews we discovered that the term 'commitment' was fairly rare in everyday speech; some couples used it only after we introduced it. This may be insignificant, but it may also be indicative that people do not always 'extract' a notion of commitment from their wider feelings of love and attachment. Thus it may not be a separate ethical value, or it may develop and take shape over time, perhaps especially in the face of difficulties. Indeed, it is arguably rather hard to claim commitment at the start of a relationship since there may have been no opportunity for it to arise or in which it could be appropriately identified. So it seemed too mechanical to think of commitment simply as a kind of oath of allegiance and instead what emerged were different accounts which entwined various feelings of love, expectations for the future, companionship, care, sexual passion, a shared history and loyalty. We identified three slightly different kinds of accounts about the decision to have a ceremony or CP. The first can be seen in terms of transformatory love, where commitment is a promise for the future. In this form commitment becomes a deeply symbolic act, an endorsement that looks ahead to a new life in partnership. The second takes the form of affirming an unfolding and shared past in which both love and commitment are embedded in ordinary everyday activities, which may not appear 'special' to the outside observer but are integral to the lives of the couple. The third is where the relationship is seen as potentially fragile and in need of some kind of external support or recognition and where a public ceremony is seen as a potential protection against disintegration. This third category can overlap with either the first or the second, and the first type can, in time, merge into the second, so these are not rigidly bounded categories. However, these accounts do throw light on how couples perceive commitment and it becomes clear that in everyday language love provides the motivation to risk committing to a relationship.

Love as transformative

I have described this future-oriented commitment as an 'act', usually a speech act, where a couple promise to be committed to one another in the future and that promise is based upon the experience of falling in love and feeling the other person to be 'the one'.

> Richard: She put the rings on first and then the binding of the hands and then we had to drink from the goblet and break bread and eat just a little bit of bread and then that was passed around everybody present. And then at the end of the ceremony you have to jump over a broomstick. What happened just before that was she actually swept away our old lives symbolically and then we stepped over the broomstick to symbolize our new lives together and that was the ceremony.

Richard and Will had been together for sixteen months when we interviewed them and they both spoke within the terms of a romantic narrative, having fallen in love at first sight. Their ceremony borrowed extensively from much older forms of informal marriage and clearly carried the symbolism of making a new life together and embarking together on a new journey of intimacy and love.

For Aaron and his partner it was slightly different because they had been together for three years when we interviewed them, but they had been in San Francisco in 2004 when same-sex marriage was briefly made legal by the mayor of the city (Kendell, 2006). So they decided to join the rush and got swept up in the emotion of the ceremony. This had a kind of transformative effect on them, as if the ceremony created a sense of love which could then be more readily articulated than before.

> Aaron: And I think it just kind of started out we need this piece of paper the document you know what I mean but once I was there it was so emotional like it was love; it was love, love, love. [. . .] And so then it became real you know it was a wedding and I have got a wedding album and photographs and newspaper cuttings and then we kind of realized that we were not just doing it for, you know, for the government legal reasons but we were doing it out of love, for emotional [reasons] and that became really quite important to us as well you know.

Although Aaron got his cheque back when the Supreme Court in the USA deemed same-sex marriage in California to be unconstitutional, he said it made no difference to their feelings. For him the ceremony had given voice to both his love and his commitment to his partner, but this was still in the form of a promise for the future. For such couples, mostly getting married quite early on in their relationships, the ceremony and the act of promising was itself transformative. Phil seems to have stepped through the looking glass into a different world, one that is typically captured in narratives of 'falling in love' and in which there is a heightened intensity generated by a decision to make a mutual commitment.

> **Phil**: And now I realize that Colin is my man, he is the man of my life, and I want to share my life with him and I tell him that regularly. And it just does not feel enough at the moment and I just want to show it in front of everyone. I just want to tell everyone he is my man, I want to be with him. So all of a sudden I am starting to like marriage which I would never thought that would happen.

Out of the fifty-four stories of same-sex marriage that we collected, approximately twelve fell into this category, namely where love was transformative and commitment was seen as a promise for the future.

The idea that a ritual or ceremony could be itself transformative is an important element in these accounts. Making vows in the presence of others, sometimes involving a deity, can have a wide range of effects. In sociological terms perhaps the most powerful is the process of 'naming', which gives an almost tangible reality to things previously felt or intuited or known in a rather ill-defined way. Even among the couples who had been together for many years and who therefore belonged to the 'commitment as process' category noted that the ceremony had made a difference to them.

> **Sally**: But on the more serious side I did feel differently afterwards I don't know what did, I'll try and describe to you. It was like we had, sort of, it was nothing tangible, but it was like something had sort of passed between us that made us belong more really. I mean now I don't really feel any different although it is still nice to know that we have done it. I am so glad we have done it. You know, I suppose in a way, in a very obvious way, it is something you have shared although we share every day of our lives together and everything else.

Commitment as a future-oriented promise can of course be treated cynically because it is often based on hope more than experience, and because the promise is untested. But this is to misunderstand the different temporal elements that can apply in the making of commitments. There is a sense in which commitment has to start somewhere. Some couples chose a precise moment for a ceremony which could be recognized by family and/or community. There are of course other 'moments' at which commitment can be said to have started, for example moving in together. But such acts do not inevitably indicate commitment in the way that a marriage does: people may buy or share homes without intending to express the kind of commitment associated with love and a long-term relationship. So, an event like getting a joint mortgage is often referred to in hindsight as a moment when a couple threw their lot in together, but few would say at the time of signing the document in their solicitor's office that it carried all the cultural meanings associated with a wedding.

It is important also to remember that these couples celebrated their partnerships before there were any legal benefits to be gained by doing so. To gain any 'real' legal protections they had to take additional, separate steps such as making legal wills in each other's favour, or arranging powers of attorney. In some sense therefore these ceremonies were 'pure' statements of both love and commitment since neither partner had anything really to gain in a material or legal sense.

Love and commitment as a relational process

For these couples (thirty-seven of the fifty-four accounts) commitment was seen as something they had clearly achieved over time, that had really grown by stealth and had often been arrived at a long time before their ceremony. The majority of these couples had been living together a considerable time, nearly all over five years, some as long as thirty years and in one case more than forty years. Their accounts were very different from those of the first group because they could draw upon a shared history of 'acts', events and decisions, all of which could be compiled to provide empirical weight to their claim to be already fully committed. While the couples who were essentially promising commitment for the future relied upon stories about the strength of their love, these established couples emphasized the depth of their relationships and the importance of a shared history of both problems and pleasures. For them the ceremony itself was rarely seen as transformative or as an event that could give greater intensity to their existing relationship. They rarely spoke in a romantic register, at least not a conventionally romantic one.

> **Interviewer**: When you exchanged your rings the first time did you make any kind of vows or promises or anything like that?
>
> **Stella**: I promised to pay the credit card on demand I expect. No I do not think we did because we bought them together didn't we really? No I think it was just by sort of understanding really wasn't [it]? I do not remember doing anything.
>
> **Denise**: No I do not think we did.
>
> **Stella**: We have always been fairly informal haven't we? 'Oh, so you are not going back to your husband then? OK. I suppose you want your tea.'

Of course statements such as these raise the question of how we (as sociologists) can identify love and affection. If an interviewee does not adopt the terminology of love and romance, or does not explicitly say they love another person, may we infer it from their accounts more generally? For example, John Eekelaar and Mavis Maclean (2004) argue that the thirty-nine people they interviewed about marriage and co-habitation rarely spoke of love as a reason for their behaviour in relationships. They also point out that Jane Lewis (2001) in her major study of marriage and co-habitation did not refer to love as an element in the relationships between the couples she interviewed. Eekelaar and Maclean do not really develop this point, but seem to suggest that the lack of discussion of love is explained by respondents feeling coy about expressing their emotions or affections to an interviewer. They may be right in this assumption and it is quite possible that there are cultural expectations about what may or may not be said in certain contexts. However, it may also be due to a limitation on the part of those sociologists who feel that they can assume that 'love' exists only when that word is articulated. For example, it is possible to read the brief exchange between Stella and Denise as a rather mundane description of imperfectly remembered events. But it can also be understood as being saturated with 'love', even though neither narrator uses the word. It helps of course to read the whole transcript of this interview, which reveals that the first time they bought rings together was pretty uneventful, but they later had a full ceremony with a registrar, using the vows used in civil weddings, and a reception at a hotel. But still their account is far from classically romantic:

> Stella: No I certainly did not feel the need to have sort of tangible evidence really. It did not matter to me in that sense. What is nice is having the certificate though.
> Denise: Yes that is very nice.
> Stella: That is nice; that means far more to me than any rings or necklaces or whatever else you give. It is nice to have the certificate and the photographs; that is far more important.
> [. . .]
> Interviewer: Did you feel differently after the ceremony about your relationship? Has it changed things?
> Denise: I don't know, I suppose because we have been together so long anyway.
> Stella: You know I am like an old shirt, yes.
> Denise: An old shoe.

Denise and Stella also described periods of stress (because Denise was applying to stay in the UK) followed by illness caused by that stress. This shared history was a story of how they cared for and showed love to one another in practical ways. This suggests that the idea of commitment as process is interwoven with the idea of love as process. Love can come to be expressed in very small acts which accumulate and become imbued with specific meanings over time. These small acts (or descriptions of small acts) and terms of endearment (being called an old shoe) may fall beneath the sociological radar because their meaning is not always transparent and it is essential to have the context of the statement or the sense is lost. What is more, love expressed in this way is not transcendent in the sense of being experienced as a removal from the mundane or everyday into a special place (Langford, 1999: 17). This might have been the kind of love expressed by Phil or Richard, but it is far removed from the kind of love expressed by Denise and Stella, for whom love is measured both in ordinary things and through understatement.

Returning to the point raised by Eekelaar and Maclean, that people do not mention 'love' as a reason for doing things in relationships, it is important to realize that the lack of such statements does not belie the fact that love is often the motivation for even the most routine of activities. It seems quite possible that the longer couples have been together, the more likely they are not to mention love overtly and the more likely they are to rely on shared histories than future intentions to explain their commitments. The couples in these long-term relationships (especially the very long ones) just took for granted that they were 'life partners' because they had travelled so far together. And although few were conventionally romantic, many spoke of the ways in which they reinvested in their relationship, often in small ways.

> **Brenda**: And I guess there are lots of ways in which we constantly cement our relationship. And yes we have given each other rings and presents at various times and as you get older and your hands get more arthritic and your knuckles get – well you have to have a new wedding ring. I mean I have got through several.
> **Joy**: I buried this one when I planted potatoes once and dug it up [again] in the autumn.
> **Stewart**: I think that because we have been together for twenty-two years [. . .] there have been enormously important moments of committing ourselves to each other when there have been sort of life crises and bereavement and things like that, that a gesture like exchanging rings does not seem as important and it is also quite material.

These are examples of how commitment and love both accumulate over time, often through small daily acts or due to sharing major life events. In some instances it was because one partner had been ill that the decision was taken to have a ceremony, while others, for example

Grace and June, chose to celebrate the twenty-fifth anniversary of their being together in this way. These marriages were a confirmation of the past and present rather than predominantly a promise for the future. This in turn was related to the fact that these couples tended to assume that the future of their relationship was already known, in other words they would be together until death parted them. The wedding ceremony in these cases could not take the form of a rite of passage in the way that it might for younger couples or for those who were only just starting to live together.

Thus, when long-term couples said that they married for pragmatic reasons (e.g. in order to acquire legal rights or to achieve equality with heterosexuals), it seems problematic to take this at face value if in so doing it is assumed that pragmatism or self-interest reigns rather than commitment or love. Legal rights and equality were naturally important to our couples (especially issues to do with inheritance, migration or acquiring the status of next of kin) but these goals might seem instrumental or self-serving if they are not contextualized within an understanding of the achievement of long-term commitment and love. In other words, when some of these couples said that they 'married' to safeguard pension entitlement or to ensure inheritance rights, it would be a misinterpretation to regard this as selfish, individualistic or solely rights-oriented. The legal contract may have been pragmatic, but the meaning of the ceremony belonged to another level of understanding. The narratives provided by these long-term couples were, in a sense, enfolded in love even if they did not use the word, and even though love was rarely expressed in a conventional, romantic vocabulary. Typically these couples felt that they had done 'the romantic thing' years before, their on-going relationships combining love, friendship and companionship, support and care.

Commitment and love in need of external support

Only three of our couples fell squarely into this category, in which the talk was about a need for external or articulated reinforcement to secure the relationship or as having a ceremony to add a dimension of security. Fourteen other couples spoke of similar needs but in more muted tones. This meant that for couples encountering difficulties in their relationships, getting married was seen as a way of helping them to weather the storm or heal a rift:

> **Hanna**: And it was at a time when we were going through a lot of difficulties weren't we? It was quite shaky actually – over issues of parenting and health issues. So Alice [. . .] suggested just a private thing, just the two of us to get these rings on our fingers, before we escaped from each other (laughing) and although I wanted [. . .] my day with a kind of dress on and things, I thought 'Yes, alright, let's do it' and then we could have a ceremony later sometime in the future so we could have a second marriage with friends and family. So we did, we had a private marriage ceremony and that was two years ago.

Others felt it necessary to marry in order to overcome problems associated with immigration or with living apart because their careers were in different places. The idea of allowing commitment to emerge over years was seen as risky: these couples felt that their relationship might not survive long without some kind of external support. For them the ceremony and the vows were like an external adhesive to help them bond the long-term relationship they wanted. And for some there was a sense that they wanted others to witness their vows not simply as a statement of love or of politics, but in order to make real or tangible what had hitherto been private promises. It was as if making public their commitment meant that there would be an external check on impulses to abandon the relationship during the hard times. This felt and expressed need for a degree of community recognition of commitment was not expected. It revealed a need for connectedness with others, as well as with established ways of conducting relationships, which fits uncomfortably with ideas about free-floating, easily abjured modern relationships which last only as long as they are mutually convenient. Lynn Jamieson et al. (2002) found similar sentiments in their study of co-habitation and commitment among young heterosexual couples in Scotland. They discovered that while for some couples commitment was established through simply living together or by being 'in love', there were others for whom getting married signified a stronger commitment and increased security. It is interesting that they found couples who believed marriage to signify greater commitment were willing to concede that this was not the case for everyone. In other words, they were not expressing what they thought was a universal moral standard relating to marriage as the pre-eminent mode of establishing commitment. Rather they expressed a personal preference, while acknowledging that this view did not hold true for others. This is an important insight because it shows that it is possible for people to achieve and/or express commitment in different ways without there being a presumption that some ways are intrinsically better than others. The same-sex couples in our study had different ways of achieving, expressing and securing their commitment. It is increasingly evident that those who dispense with conventional forms are not necessarily dispensing with commitment. They found modes of expression which related to the interiority of their relationships as well as to their wider values and the significance of other relationships. They had choices, but these were relational in context. For some a deity was also part of the equation:

> **Sam**: I cannot remember; was it the autumn that we first moved in here after a bit more than a year of living together that we were engaged? Well I think pretty early on we sort of, because of the Christian thing and because of all the numerous issues that came up with that, and we talked about being committed to each other and in the eyes of God quite early. [. . .] Yes I think we have made our commitment in the eyes of God.

These kinds of narrative reveal as problematic the presumptions often found in accounts of individualization, that people are increasingly self-referential and autonomous. Even those in our sample who did not see marriage as a source of external support or security wanted family and friends to know about their ceremonies and to participate with them in recognizing the significance of their relationship. Only two couples opted for entirely private events with no one else present. And so the overwhelming majority of these ceremonies were essentially relational events set within networks of friends and family.

* * *

In this chapter I have reflected on empirical data and quoted extensively from transcribed interviews because it seems important to convey the various meanings that individuals and couples were constructing around their partnership ceremonies and the associated issues of love and commitment. It becomes apparent that to separate commitment from love in intimate relationships is problematic: they work together, the one involves the other. Separating them can lead to a presumption that commitment is the good and/or worthy moral stance while love is unreliable and/or ephemeral, an optional extra subordinate to the stalwart obligations implicit in the concept of commitment. A focus solely on commitment reduces the individual to a one-dimensional being, cognizant only of duty, and it robs the person of precisely the realm of the 'magical' and transformatory which imbues much of daily life with meaning. While Gergen's insistence that emotions 'constitute social life itself' refers to many more emotions than are contained in the constellation referred to as love, this idea does acknowledge the importance of love in the sociological schema. In other words, perhaps it is time to take seriously the idea that love motivates action and association, it need not be an ideology with an underlying false promise. This in turn may challenge the view found both at the pessimistic end of individualization theories and in the popular pro-family narrative, that divorce is too easy, a sign of moral laxness and a failure to commit. But it should also prompt us into further enquiry into love relationships beyond the sexual couple (whether homosexual or heterosexual) and to consider more relationally how love works across a range of relationships, for example with friends (Allan, 1989; Jamieson, 1998) or among siblings. Mauthner, for example, discusses how relationships between sisters are often taken for granted. Notwithstanding their significance throughout many women's private lives, they can be socially invisible:

> Unlike motherhood, marriage and 'the family', relationships between biological sisters lack their own institutions or representations in the public sphere. This raises difficulties for describing a tie that exists primarily in the private realm of domestic life with no language, public discourse or images of its own. (2005: 14)

These kinds of ties speak of sociability, intimacies, close contact, shared memories and shared biographies. These qualities and experiences are the antithesis of the popular concept of needy selfish strangers. But if we can retrieve love and positive emotions from the cynical aura of some strands of the individualization thesis, it still remains to acknowledge that some emotions may be negative and hurtful, and that even love where it is reciprocated can co-reside with inequalities of gender, wealth, age, health and so on. If we no longer accept the idea that love is impossible where there are inequalities, then it becomes important to consider how these apparently competing forces manage to co-exist. Studies of money management in heterosexual relationships, discussed in chapter 7, show clearly how inequalities (around income) are delicately negotiated in the context of preserving a valued relationship. Negative emotions have to be negotiated too and these in particular are subject to the influences of gender and generational power, as explored fully in chapter 6. In this chapter, however, I make no excuses for dwelling on positive emotions if only because these are vital threads in the fabric of personal life.

4

Connections, Threads and Cultures of Tradition

Who are you when you don't know your past?

Adie, 2005

This question is the subtitle of Kate Adie's book *Nobody's Child*, which is based on her own life story and research into the situation facing 'foundlings', in other words those infants who were abandoned at birth and never reclaimed and who have little chance of finding their biological parents. Not only do they have little chance of finding their forebears, but rarely is there any information at all for them about their families of origin. The foundling, even more than the adopted child, has come to symbolize the ontologically at-risk being who, on attaining an age where these things might start to matter, is predicted to face a kind of biographical black hole which is capable of derailing an ordinary life course. The (varied) feelings and experiences that Adie describes point to the practical and bureaucratic difficulties that can arise when an individual has no 'real' family history, but also encompass the sense of isolation and disconnectedness that can accompany the discovery that one's biography starts abruptly at birth, with no antecedents or inherited memories and memorabilia (Carsten, 2000).

For many the sense of being embedded in a family history can be taken for granted and, as a result, it may go unremarked. For refugees, orphans, adoptees and the displaced these issues are more likely to loom large. It has become a conventional wisdom that familial roots which can locate a person emotionally, genetically and culturally are essential for ontological security and a sense of self. Yet at the same time, in a kind of parallel universe, it is argued that in post-modern conditions we make our own selves and biographies, and that we have become the authors (if not heroes) of our own lives. The self is seen as malleable, dependent on context and open to being rewritten by the author of any given autobiography (Brison, 1997). It is not my intention to establish whether one version or another of the construction of the self is 'correct', since I argue that these are ultimately compatible;[1] rather I seek to understand how people in families weave these threads or webs of tradition and connection that become a kind of security blanket for those who can take for granted a cultural past and hence an embeddedness with what has gone before.

This chapter therefore starts by looking at the ideas and concepts that have been developed in thinking about social memory and the place of cultural narratives. I then move on to more substantive terrain to explore family practices which are explicitly about creating traditions (and embeddedness in traditions); this involves understanding how the present is actively rooted in the past, which in turn provides the foundation for Adie's question: 'Who are you when you don't know your past?'

The past in the present

Telling stories is central to social identifications.

Blokland, 2005: 126

I too desire to participate in the identity of my parents.

Edwards, 2000: 18, following Strathern

Talya Blokland's interests are in social memory, while Jeanette Edwards is a social anthropologist who has studied the nature of kinship. Despite these differences in approach, I see these two epigraphs as conceptual bookends for a set of related ideas on the fabric of meaningful, personal connections. Blokland's remark points to the significance of narrative practices which create intelligible accounts of past or present events and in which people can situate themselves, either by recognizing similarities (of self or of experience) or by identifying difference. Blokland argues that this process is productive of 'social identifications' a term used instead of the more usual 'identity' in order to capture the processual and even unfinishedness of acquiring and moulding a sense of self in given contexts. But she is also stressing that story-telling is a social activity, not simply in the sense that it involves at least two people – teller and listener – but in that it produces sociability and socialness through connecting people at the level of shared (or comparable) imaginings and experiences. Stories told among families are often used quite consciously as ways of trying to share experiences across generations, whether to offer moral guidance or to assist a child in understanding incidents and observations he or she may encounter beyond the home (Brannen et al., 2004). Equally, stories may be 'simply' historical, which is to say recollections of childhood summers (happy times), or of bereavement, or of problems encountered and overcome. Telling stories of one's childhood to one's children is a common activity and through that mechanism threads or links are created across generations.

In their study of four generations of families in the USA, Vern Bengtson et al. (2002) borrow the concept of 'linked lives' from G. H. Elder Jr. (1994), through which they argue that the lives of family members are linked in various ways (shared homes, overlapping biographies, shared genes and so on). But this concept does not necessarily require an actual, temporal or physical link if we expand it to consider the work that is done by story-telling. Thus a grandparent or parent telling stories of her or his childhood links a child to a time that is past, but also to a being who no longer exists in the same form. It is an imaginary link, but profoundly meaningful nonetheless. Similarly links may be made with relatives who are no longer living. This means (to return to Blokland's observation) that identifications are made in the present but based on stories of times long past. It is of course possible that stories told in childhood will fade and become less significant as a child grows older, but they have a habit of resurfacing later in life, particularly with the onset of parenthood. So these stories can be submerged and become less influential, but they have the capacity to be revived when the next generation is being drawn into the family narrative.

Blokland's work on memory allows us to think beyond the practice of story-telling, however, because she links this process with the formation of a sense of self. Furthermore, Blokland reminds us that story-telling is not an innocent activity. What is remembered is always selected: the reason a story is told relates specifically to the current context and the current audience. Blokland's work focuses on social memories in a working-class community. She argues that the telling of stories is part of the social process of inclusion and exclusion, as well as part of the operations of power. Arguably this holds for families too, since – as I discuss in chapter 5 – not everyone is told the same stories; different family members may receive different versions of the same events. But I now go on to focus on the way in which story-telling can be a practice of inclusion or inscription (Connerton, 1994: 72): it builds a shared history and shared ancestry which makes the 'new' generation belong (even if they feel uncomfortable or ultimately rebel). It is these threads and links that Adie identifies as missing when she asks how you can know who you are without knowing your past.

The telling of stories in families might carry greater significance than community-based stories because the stories told concern people who are kin and who are socially positioned as significant, perhaps even sharing certain character traits, personalities, aptitudes, body types and so on. Moreover, as Clive Seale (2000) has put it: 'Through narrative constructions of our personal biographies we formulate self-identities embedded in social networks, whose currency is that of emotional exchange' (2000: 41). He argues that there is an emotional component because these kinds of narrative not only express emotions, but are part of building emotional links and bonds. He goes on to discuss how this emotional, intersubjective communication also embodies an ethic because we feel pleasure in reciprocation and a sense of shame if bonds, once established, are broken. In family narratives, therefore, not only are emotional bonds created (Lieberman, 1979), but also a sense of duty or a sense of doing 'the proper thing'. These bonds are created in the broad context of class, ethnicity and gender and so should not be seen as isolated from wider practices. Such narratives may create bonds to a particular class fraction, locality, or ethnic group as well as family (e.g. Hoffman, 2005). The stories may be highly gendered, for example bonding girls to their mothers and boys to fathers. In this way we can understand how the creation of emotional bonds 'inside' families can be interwoven with wider social bonds and practices.

Seale's introduction of emotions into this discussion is vital because family relationships are nothing if not permeated with every imaginable kind of feeling. Thus the telling of stories in families can be acts of affection (stressing someone's good qualities), or of loathing (applauding the banishment of the scapegoat). But these narratives of emotion are not simply an expression of internally generated, idiosyncratic feelings, they are scripted in a relational context and the emotion expresses a normative stance which is often shared by other members of the family. As Andrew Sayer argues: 'Emotions are not a redundant accompaniment to the business of life, like muzak in a supermarket, but commentaries which relate to our concerns and evaluations of the import of things' (2005: 36).

This means that, as I argue in chapter 3, we need to incorporate an understanding of emotions in our analysis of what families do, not just because people experience and express emotions routinely, but because the emotions expressed are sociologically significant. Consider the following account from an interview I carried out as part of a project on kinship after divorce.[2] It comes from a grandparent whose son-in-law had defrauded her daughter, leaving her with huge debts and ultimately homeless. He subsequently spent time in prison. On his release he wrote to his former wife asking about his two sons.

> **Grandmother**: And [he was] just more or less asking how they were really, you know, and she said she didn't know what to do. So she said 'Shall I tell Michael I've had a letter?' so I said 'I think you should. He's eight; he is old enough to know.' So she told him and he got really upset and he wanted to see his dad. So he said could [he] write him a letter, so she said yes, so he wrote his dad a letter.

But she didn't post it. She just felt that she didn't want them to have contact. Because like she said at the time, he was living in Cardiff, she said there is no way he is coming to my house to see them and there is no way I would let them go to Cardiff, because she was frightened that she would never see them again, she had that fear that if he got his hands on them he would take them off, she would never see them again. So there was no way she was gonna let them go to him in Cardiff; by the same token there was no way she was gonna have him in her house, so she didn't want them to have that contact you see. But then she decided she would. Oh, she got a letter from the CSA to say that he'd agreed to pay maintenance so she said 'Oh well if he's gonna start being committed to them I will let him see them.' But he never paid his maintenance.

This passage is full of emotions, values, characterizations, doubts, justifications, vindications, and sadness. Although this grandmother was staunchly on the side of the 'wronged' daughter, as was the grandfather, their loyalty was also to their grandchildren and particularly the older boy's right to know his father. They are caught up in a family drama because the grandmother's advice is required ('Shall I tell Michael?'), but when the advice is followed there is an adverse outcome. The emotional response of the little boy is 'managed' through a deceit and he is left to imagine that his dad simply never responded to his letter. The grandmother is unsure about the ethics of this 'solution'. Her daughter is restored to an ethical position, however, because she relents over allowing her son to see his dad when it appears that the father will pay child support – thus showing that he is committed to the children. However, in the end, everything reverts to the norm because the father shows his 'true colours' by failing to pay child support and so the mother's original stance is vindicated.

While this is an account of one particular family, the issues discussed are common to many families where there has been a divorce or separation and where competing loyalties and interests are at stake. So while it involves individual lives, experienced personally, in being recounted at the start of the twenty-first century it is also very much 'of its time'. The emotions expressed carry social significance (any upset over a child who cannot see his or her father raises ethical issues about contact) but these emotions and stories are also being expressed by many parents and grandparents in the West at precisely the same time and thus these accounts constitute a social phenomenon.

Returning to the second epigraph to this section ('I too desire to participate in the identity of my parents') we can shift towards a related set of issues about connectedness and embeddedness. Edwards is moved to make this remark in the context of kinship having introduced her book *Born and Bred* with a brief biographical note on her own childhood. In her account Edwards positions herself as the daughter of hard-working, meagerly educated working-class parents (who were in turn the children of working-class parents with large numbers of children). Her parents strove to improve the situation for their family, to gain better housing, to leave the city for a suitable place to bring up children, and to give their children more opportunities than they had had. Edwards's story is far from unique, but she is astute in recognizing that her narrative, which locates her inside this story, is the reflection of a desire to be part of her parents' identity – a compelling insight. In other words, Edwards tells the reader about herself by telling us about her parents; she tells us about their kind so that we will recognize the stamp of person she is. But she does this knowingly and reflects upon the process. The point of Edwards's main argument is that the past is part of the present; it permeates the present and helps to shape it both practically and conceptually. So we use the past, we resort to it knowingly and unknowingly, it frames and contextualizes the ways in which we negotiate the present and the future. Through Edwards's discussion we can begin to understand why the past, particularly the past we are closely or personally linked to through kinship, becomes meaningful and also why we can become inextricably attached to it. Edwards's personal account, and the accounts of the people she interviewed in Bacup, Lancashire, show how connections are remade in the telling of the present and how, almost automatically, we embed ourselves in our heritage when describing ourselves in the present. It is small wonder that some of the people that Adie interviewed felt cut adrift, given their position in a culture whose routine narrative practice entails this recourse to heritage.

In this discussion so far I have attempted to draw together a number of threads which have already been identified by other authors. These include the social significance of narratives, particularly family narratives; the process of identifications achieved through narrative; the significance of the past and particularly how the past lives of parents and other kin (linked lives) become sedimented into family stories and traditions and even ways of knowing and seeing; the place of emotion in the telling of stories that make bonds become even stronger; and finally the moral significance of expressed emotions. I now aim to trace these threads through some of the stories told to me by the parents of mixed heritage children. These parents have a particular awareness of difference (their own past experiences compared with their partner's) and have to negotiate quite explicitly which elements of their own heritage they wish to transmit to their children. For them nothing can be taken for granted because, for example, a Jewish mother married to an atheist from a Protestant background cannot simply assume that her children will be Jewish; she will have to negotiate an outcome which is attentive to difference.

The study I rely upon here was a small-scale investigation involving in-depth interviews with parents in six families (in the end this comprised five couples and one individual because the latter's partner did not wish to participate).[3] All of the couples had children, as this was a key element in selection, and all had partnered (since not all had married) across some kind of cultural 'boundary', whether 'race', religion or nationality or all of these. The point was to try to capture people who brought with them rather different backgrounds into their partnership and parenthood in order to see how (and indeed whether) they imparted their own cultural heritage to their children. The working presumption of this study was not that these parents would operate in entirely different ways compared with parents who shared similar backgrounds, but that they would just be more aware of the processes they were going through and thus more able to articulate their stories.

There is no assumption here that these parents represent anybody but themselves, nor that they are typical, nor even that they are extraordinary. It will become apparent from their accounts that although some came originally from poor or migrant backgrounds, most had become professionals or at least benefited from comfortable economic and cultural resources.

Couple 1   Doug was a white man in his mid-fifties, born and brought up in West London. He had no particular religious faith but went to a Church of England school. His father (who was Jewish) died when he was a teenager, but his mother had no religious faith at all. His partner Mavis was New York Jewish. They had two teenage sons. Doug's mother was still alive but in a nursing home, Mavis's mother was still living in the USA but her father died after she married Doug.

Couple 2   Brigit's family was originally from British Guyana but she was born in the UK. Her family were Methodists and her parents live with her and her husband. Brigit lived in the US for several years where she met and married Henry, who was from a liberal Bostonian, Jewish background. They had two children together, and Henry had a child by an earlier marriage. Both followed their different religious faiths actively.

Couple 3   Maria had an Italian mother and a Jamaican father and her parents were separated, with her mother living with her and her family for six months each year. Jim was of Jamaican origin but brought up in London. Both were staunch church-goers and members of the Pentecostal congregation. Between them they had nine children. Both also came from very large families.

Couple 4   Sita was in her forties and came originally from Delhi. Her parents had rejected both religion and caste for political reasons, but her cultural milieu was Brahmin and Hindu. Jonathon was Anglo-Irish, and identified as Irish. His family were Protestant. Both Sita and Jonathon had moved to England when they were adults and met at university. They had two sons under ten at the time of the interview.

Couple 5   Eleanor was in her late fifties and was New York Jewish. She had family in the US but her parents had died. Patrick was English, from the Home Counties, and described as a lapsed Catholic. Both were living in Scotland and they had one son of their relationship and Patrick had a son by his first marriage. Patrick's parents were still living.

Couple 6 Helen was in her late forties and of a white middle-class background; her father's occupation had made her widely travelled as a child. Andrew was Black British, born in Jamaica and educated in the UK. Both came from a strong Church of England background but did not subscribe to a faith. They had four children and parents on both sides were still living at the time of the interview.

In order to pull together the threads identified above I now draw on different parts of our interviews with these parents and discuss them in the following four sections. The first addresses the ways in which the parents locate themselves in their own biographical and cultural histories, while the second is concerned with ways in which parents construct a meaningful past for their children by telling stories of their own pasts. The third explores the cultural practices and ceremonies which celebrate and relive aspects of the parents' pasts and how these are part of the process of creating emotional and moral bonds. And finally I turn to what these parents hope to have achieved by this whole process, and how they see the formation of their children's identities.

Connectedness, biography and the self

The parents in this study had no difficulty in locating themselves or, to use Blokland's term, in expressing their identifications. This entailed a number of cultural indicators with condensed meanings, some of which needed careful decoding. Because of the importance of locating oneself in a narrative history, I quote below from almost all the parents we interviewed; not only because what they say is testimony to a wide range of different biographies, but because the biographic signifiers commonly used vary in significance and intensity even if the narratives they provide usually take a similar, and familiar, form.

Henry: My cultural background, I'm an American Jew or a Jewish American, I haven't quite decided which. Err, very strong, well in terms of my grandparents [who] had immigrated from Eastern Europe to the States. My parents were both born in the States. A classical immigrant thing where the grandparents all work, their children then went to university and then everybody, you know, each generation moved up the ladder as it were. And that's it in a nutshell I guess.

Brigit: My background is that I was born in what was then British Guyana, so it was a British colony. So my parents' ideal was that, you know, England was the mother country and that was the place to go and to raise your children. So my father, he wasn't quite *Windrush*, he was like a year or two after the *Windrush*.[4] [. . .] Faith-wise – we've always been Methodists, we've never been anything else but Methodists and that's just because – that's what – for generations, the grandparents way back were Methodists.

Doug: Yes [my background] would be, it would be West London, but no religious influence whatsoever. But a lot of immigrants and people of different faiths, all the way through. School friends, which I'm still friendly with, of all different faiths. Some religious, some not.

Mavis: [My] background – I'm a first generation American and I do still consider, you know even though I live here, I am still an American, obviously, Er and basically you know, Jewish American. And yes I'd probably put the Jewish first, rather than the American first. Because the Jewishness follows me, and it is very cultural. You know I grew up, in New York, basically in a totally Jewish neighbourhood. Everybody was Jewish, you only saw Christians [. . .] somewhere else.

Sita: My father is an economist, my mother is a political historian and both of them are atheists. Both of them had participated in the Nationalist Movement and also the left movement which grew out of the Nationalist Movement. [. . .] Both of them came from what is now Pakistan so they lived through the partition of India and therefore knew loss in terms of homeland but were very lucky because neither of their families suffered physical damage. My mother's family was very well off I think in Punjab. My grandfather was very highly educated.

Jonathon: My father came from an Anglo-Irish family, I think, so what marked them out when they were living in the South [of Ireland] was the fact that they wouldn't go to a Catholic church. They'd go to the Church of Ireland church so things would kick in there about identity and, when we were living in Northern Ireland, I think the combination of having an English mother who also was of no religion [. . .] and my father who also didn't give it much credence – but I also knew that I wasn't Catholic. So there was kind of a no man's land almost if you like between, and maybe there's also a class thing that kicks in here. There were certain choices that came in that might not have been available if I'd been working class.

Maria: I just had a mixture of Italian and Jamaican really. Sort of even mix of both. [. . .] And so you know there was my dad with all his family and his culture and there's my mother with all her family and culture. They both come from very big families. My mum comes from six and my dad comes from twelve. So it's a lot of family. They were both very, they were both, you know different. The values were different.

Interviewer: Could you say a bit more about what you mean by being raised in a very – your background being very Jamaican – I mean what does that mean?

Jim: Well I suppose in terms of the views, because my parents brought me up very much the way they were brought up and obviously they were brought up in Jamaica. Their standards, their expectations in behaviour, in attitude which are different I guess than general British kind of behaviour. [. . .] I would never answer back. Whatever my thoughts were I would keep them to myself and I'd mumble it later, out of earshot, you know. And that's the way we were brought up. We were brought up that way that any adults who spoke to us we didn't answer them back. Which you know, is not what I see now.

Eleanor: Sometimes I would describe myself as Jewish and sometimes I would describe myself as American – but American is more a nationality whereas Jewish more of ethnic tag. So probably Jewish.

Interviewer: And what about your partner – how would you describe him?

Eleanor: Er I would just call him English. He's terribly English [laughter]. You'll see.

Helen: As a young child [I] lived in New Zealand for a while and then when Dad was in the forces we lived in France and Belgium for a while and I went to a convent and this kind of thing. But then we just kept moving all of the time [. . .] but we moved around a lot up here; probably lived in about five places around here so I see here as kind of home. Yeah home, if there is one, is around this part of the North.

There are a number of common themes in these short extracts, notwithstanding the significant variations in ethnicity, social class, politics and religion (or absence of religion). Each person stresses something slightly different, for example education rather than religion, ethnicity rather than nationality, place rather than family. Almost everyone appears to have a prepared or well-rehearsed account since there were few hesitations in the interviews. All the stories that these individuals told started with, or included at some stage, an outline of their parents' lives. Sometimes grandparents were also mentioned as anchor points for their own parents' trajectories. All these individuals had either migrated or moved or were living with someone whose family had migrated; this appears to have created an awareness of the significance of place. This is not 'place' in a purely spatial or geographical sense, but place in the sense of locations associated with specific meanings and imbued with history. For some it created a sense of 'out-of-placeness', which led to debates about 'return' or at least a sense of yearning for something they were missing. There were also shorthand references to symbolically significant historical or cultural events which shaped a particular biography. For example Brigit's reference to the *Windrush* evokes a cluster of meanings around migration from the West Indies into a grim, cold and profoundly racist post-war Britain in 1948. Helen also spoke of her partner's parents' departure from Jamaica in the 1950s to come to England to find work, leaving Andrew behind with relatives. Sita mentions her parents' living through the partition between Pakistan and India with a fleeting allusion to the politics and violence of the time. Elsewhere there are references to 'placelessness' because the family kept moving around the world with the father's job. In Helen's case the lack of a special place is made up for by the creation of meaning around a city in the North which was made into 'home'.

These examples cannot convey the complexities of the iden-tifications that these parents made. Some flavour of this, however, is captured in references about whether to put Jewishness or American-ness first in adopting identifying labels (a point to which I return in the context of the children's identifications) or whether to sense religious identity in terms of feeling 'out-of-place' (e.g. a Protestant in the South of Ireland). Other complexities include pos-sible distinctions between the culture and cultural practices associ-ated with a faith (e.g. Hindu, Catholic or Methodist) and various levels of religious adherence. These are not necessarily fixed identifications: the individuals we interviewed recognized that what might be called 'inflections' of their overall identity might change with time, place or circumstance. However, these stories created a sedimented past on which to rely and could be seen as a stable launching pad for future identifications. It does not matter that the parents' identities might have been no less fixed than their own; what matters is the way in which the story fixes them and their lives as a (fictitious) starting point, which then apparently explained much of what ensued. Thus stories might involve saying 'My parents moved a lot so I stay still' or equally 'My parents migrated several times, so I now like to move too.' These are not 'rational' or causal explanations, but stories of emotional connection and modes of personal accounting.

Cultural stories of childhood

Sita: I was telling the children just recently when they went on this march in London, we all went, but I was saying you know my first memory of a march was on my dad's shoulders against the war in Vietnam. And here we are again.

Jonathon: [T]hey love to hear about stories of our childhoods. So Sita and I both tell the boys things that happened to us and with us early on in our lives whether it was when we were ten or twenty or whatever. They find that quite interesting. They always like to have those kinds of conversations and they ask quite a few questions arising out of it.

For these parents, telling stories about their own childhoods to their children was particularly important because they had typically experienced very different sorts of childhood, and often in quite different places, even in different countries. Sita here draws on a shared experience of political activism, which she felt herself to be passing on to her children. The moment captured her own past experiences, but she was making the present experience for her children more meaningful (for her and for them) by embroidering the occasion with reference to important, parallel events from her own childhood. She implies a circularity not only of events, but also of values – in this case an anti-war sentiment. Jonathon points to his children's enjoyment in hearing about his past and the way in which, as a family, they engage in the shared enterprise of excavating the past. The fact that these enterprises are mutually enjoyable is a core element of the exchange of both sentiment and values.

Sometimes the stories told were cultural 'fictions' or even acknowledged fables.

Henry: And I get to make the home-made cranberry sauce and tell the story of the first Thanksgiving. [laughter]
Brigit: The kids are like: 'Oh Dad for God's sake, not again! We know, we know about the bloody pilgrims.' [laughter]
Interviewer: Well at least if they wait for the next generation then they get to tell it . . .
Brigit: . . . get to tell it once and then it's the same story and it's like 'Please not again.' [laughter] But it's nice. We look forward to it.

The repetition of certain stories is a way of 'fixing' certain cultural understandings. The laughter in this account is underpinned by open expressions of enjoyment. In this way the story-telling – no matter how familiar – is imbued with affection and a sense of connectedness, both within the family and with a notion of 'American-ness'. As Barbara Misztal (2003) has pointed out, memories 'laid down' in childhood become associated with special times and special emotions and so, no matter how boring the story may become, it will carry a resonance for all the members. Ironically this particular story might have much more resonance for Henry and Brigit's children than for American children who are living in the USA. It may develop a sentimental value and have the power to evoke their childhood, precisely because it occupies such a symbolic place in memory. In other words they may well tell this story to their own children, over and over again.

Grandparents could also be important in this story-telling process, describing to their grandchildren what the children's parents had been like when they were children. Equally they might tell stories of their own childhoods, thus bridging generations and linking different places and times. Whether told by parents or grandparents, such stories could take two forms. They could be a way of filling in children's knowledge of the past or of cultural traditions, thus contributing towards making the child both part of the family (through knowledge of heritage) and part of the culture (Bertaux and Thompson, eds, 2005). They might, however, be used deliberately to teach children about the wider world or to give them skills and knowledge about managing life's events.

> **Jonathon**: I think I'm doing a number of things [when I tell stories]. I think I want them to know about me to some extent – about where I've come from. I suspect also that lots of things trigger the stories but I'm sure some of the time there's some moral to the story that I want to tell them here and now. This sounds awful! I hope it's not that bad in real life [laughter] because the stories might illustrate being judgemental or being weak or frailty or injustice or something humorous or absurd. The stories have very different purposes or say very different things but I know it is about wanting to tell them about who I am. I know that and what I believe in, and sometimes the stories I tell them will be rooted in my childhood and sometimes they will be much more recent. But it's a very marked feature, well I say it's a very marked feature of our family life but I don't know whether it's that different in other family lives. I suspect maybe it's not. I don't know.

Jonathon identifies the 'moral agenda' of story-telling in families which runs alongside the desire to let his children get to know him through this narrative device. He demonstrates that it is not enough for his children to know him as he is in the present and through his relationship to them as father, he wants them to know him as he once was (or at least as he now recalls himself to have been). But he equally wants the narrative to be a way of sharing wisdom[5] and giving his children the indirect 'experience' of events, problems and conflicts which they may not yet have encountered for themselves.

Cultural practices of childhood

Of equal significance to story-telling could be the re-enactment of rituals and ceremonies of childhood for the next generation. For most of the adults in this study, such rituals had lost significance once they had left home; indeed, some described rebelling against them in their teen years. But on becoming parents these abandoned practices could be resurrected – sometimes warmly, sometimes with ambivalence but nonetheless they were restored into the routine of family practices.

> **Mavis**: I, I mean suppose when we came back and err, well as I said the whole thing comes back to having your children. All of a sudden you realize that you want to give them, you know, the joy and trad-ition of what you grew up with and carry it on.

> **Eleanor**: And then when we had our child, various rituals became more important and connections with our families of origin became more important and therefore the differences were highlighted in a way that they hadn't been before. So the production of the child is often the kind of locus, the repository, for all these cultural practices and, as our [son] grew up, we became more and more aware of these differences.

Having children was a trigger to memory as well as a reconnec-tion with events and customs which were familiar in an earlier childhood. Sita explained that she had deliberately gone against religious/cultural customs as a teenager, but had returned to the lighting of candles for Diwali once her own children were born. For the parents in this group who were not religious, such a return sometimes meant having to relearn partly recollected rituals. This could, in itself, generate renewed contact with relatives who had to be contacted for advice on how or where to acquire artefacts or religious books. Such parents obviously felt a need to re-create culture-filled, meaningful moments, which were not automatically part of their children's immediate milieu. In this way they connected with the past as well as shaped the scope of their children's family imaginary.

Because these parents came from different cultural backgrounds, faiths and places, they also had to negotiate with each other over which ceremonies or practices to restore for their children's benefit. This could be difficult, especially if what was at stake was a decision about the tradition or family that the child would be invited to identify with most strongly. Decisions about which ceremonies to include could be relatively easy as all traditions could be adhered to, but in some areas decisions could leave 'indelible' marks or could impose life-long meanings and consequences on the path the children would follow. One such decision could be choosing a name for a child; another more difficult one could be a decision about whether to circumcise a boy. I shall explore the ramifications of each of these in turn.

The naming of a child

The naming of children is almost always a defining moment but when the child is of mixed heritage the decision might have several ramifications. With three of the six couples we interviewed the naming process was complicated in that the women had assumed their husband's surname on marriage. This meant that their children took their fathers' surnames, leaving the mother (and her kin) at a 'disadvantage' in the cultural inheritance stakes. In these cases given names might be selected to reflect the 'other side' of the family. So, for example, where a mother is Jewish, Old Testament

names might be chosen; in other instances one child might be
named for one side of the family and a second child for the other.

Helen and Andrew, whose children are of white English and
Caribbean descent, decided on very 'English' names for their three
sons. This is in keeping with the Caribbean tradition, so it did not
offend either side of the extended family in any way;[6] but their
thinking was partly influenced by a feeling that their sons might
have enough to contend with in the form of racism, without having
the additional burden of unusual names. However, they chose an
African name for their daughter – much against the wishes of the
sons, who were worried that she would be singled out and ridiculed
at their very white school.

Sita and Jonathon gave their first-born son an Indian first name,
his second name being that of his Irish grandfather; their second
son has an Irish first name, his second name being that of his Indian
grandfather. In this way different traditions were honoured, while
both grandfathers were also respected. By the same token the boys
were given the combined (hyphenated) surnames of their parents as
their last name.

> **Jonathon**: They both have Indian and Irish names. We both liked the
> name and we both decided we wanted to give our [first] child an
> Indian name and then when we knew there was going to be a second
> boy we decided we wanted our child to have an Irish name. So yes
> there was a signalling in the names that these children come from
> two different traditions. [. . .] I was just thinking about [surnames]
> as well. Will the boys call themselves (by both our surnames) all their
> lives or will they drop one? And as I was thinking well they'll prob-
> ably keep them because increasingly you come across people who've
> got these double-barrelled names for the very reason that our chil-
> dren have them. Not because they're failed royals but because a par-
> ticular hybridity is being expressed. And I also thought, well I
> wonder whether they will always want to be known by those first
> names. I don't know. I haven't spoken to them about that. But I
> should raise it at some point.

The importance of a name for connectedness (with history, with
culture, with family) cannot really be overstated, especially when

family members perceive themselves to be balanced (metaphorically speaking) between the past, present and future. Names cannot simply reflect obligations to the past, however, unless the new generation are perceived as mere vehicles for transporting the past into the future. Typically they are viewed not in such one-dimensional ways, but also as people who will ultimately have to make their own way. Eleanor's comments below capture this mixture of considerations:

> **Eleanor:** And Patrick's family asked in passing whether we had any plans to baptize him and I'm not quite sure what words he used but the gist was 'Certainly not'. And so, there were questions asked, and, yeah, and the naming of the child – that's also interesting in trying to kind of marry the different communities we straddled. We tried to think of a name that would be okay with the Jewish relatives, okay with Home Counties English relatives with roots in Ireland and okay in a Scottish playground – so that's how we came up with these names.

Circumcision

Whether or not to circumcise sons posed very difficult issues for parents of Jewish heritage because, while names can be quite easily changed later in life, a circumcision cannot be reversed and, if not done in early infancy, it is a very painful procedure. For the three Jewish parents we interviewed, the question was complex not simply because their partner might be against the practice, but because they were not themselves highly religious and did not observe strict religious teaching in other areas of their lives. These parents tended to argue that they took the decision, and persuaded their partner to agree, so that their sons could participate fully in the Jewish faith later in life *if they so wished*. Circumcision was akin to leaving a cultural avenue open. It meant that the sons would be readily accepted into the faith if that choice was made, or perhaps that they would not have the painful option of a late circumcision.

> **Eleanor:** What would we do about the circumcision? Well as it happens Patrick was circumcised when he was born because that was the common practice among middle-class English people in the late

1940s. So I could justify [our son's] circumcision, so that he would look like his father. But actually we knew that the reason was because of cultural continuity. But I read all this literature about circumcision as kind of genital mutilation, the unnecessariness of it, and you know I'm completely convinced of the case that it's an unnecessary medical procedure – but I did it anyway. My one piece of resistance was that it wasn't a religious ceremony.

Eleanor spoke of the way in which her cousins and other relatives phoned her to ask about the circumcision, exerting a form of pressure. Mavis discovered that she did not really know how to go about it as she then lived in a slightly remote rural area. The Methodist Brigit, on the other hand, was totally against it; she nonetheless conceded to Henry's wishes, even though she felt that circumcision would be against her son's interests rather than create a bond with one part of his heritage.

> **Brigit**: And I had to stay in the hospital because of the fact that Henry insisted that [our son] was circumcised. And what really upset me – I mean after you have a baby you're so emotional anyway – and what really upset me was he insisted on this. [. . .] And I knew it was going to happen, and I was lying in bed doing this and I could still hear him scream. I mean, it can still bring tears to my eyes. And I ranted and raved and said 'How could you do this to our son and you weren't even there?' [. . .] And that, I think is the only time that our religion has ever been a big issue, was the fact that it affected him so profoundly. I mean I know he didn't remember it but, having said that, because his willy is different to the other boys that weren't circumcised he questioned [it] because they said his willy looked like a sausage or something. So again that affected some of his school life as well, 'cos he would be upset about that because he was different. You know so that's been a bit of an issue at times.

Brigit's account reveals the tensions that can be created in carrying on with certain customs. It is important because, notwithstanding the ways in which the six couples in this study coped with cultural difference, it is clear that trying to carry on different (sometimes opposed) cultural practices through one's children cannot only create dissent but even cause breakdown. Certain ritual practices can be said to cross an important symbolic line and can thus generate negative feelings, but circumcision was the most fraught issue among the three couples concerned, perhaps because no compromise solution is possible. All the other religious rituals and ceremonies were relatively easy to manage. Families could readily observe Christmas, Hanukkah, Diwali and/or Thanksgiving; they could light candles or eat fish on a Friday, have turkey twice a year, learn about very different gods and different religious stories and fables.

> **Doug**: It was great for the two boys you see, 'cos not only were they getting all the Christian holidays and you know the Easter eggs and the Christmas presents, they were getting the Hanukkah presents and everything.
>
> **Mavis**: That was a deal we made that Doug didn't care about any of it, just as long as we had a Christmas tree he was happy.

But circumcision was different and once the decision was made both parent and child had to live with it.

The process of creating identifications

> **Jim**: You know, for me it's about believing that there's a certain way that we should, you know, conduct ourselves and teach our children to conduct themselves and I think that transcends time anyway. I don't think time has anything to do with it. 'Cos there are some things which I think should never change.

The previous section addresses the importance of cultural heritage and its achievement through narrative and ceremony. Even though this involves invoking religious practices or stories, most of the parents in this small sample were not strongly religious, some of them showing agnostic or atheist leanings. But they all held strong moral values and part of the process of imparting cultural heritage was also about wanting their children both to share a moral lexicon with them, and also to feel bonded with them through a particular vocabulary of values – or, as Jim puts it, to find a shared way of 'conducting ourselves'. To some extent, Jim's words reflect the ideas of Bourdieu on habitus (Swartz, 1997). He wants his children to embody certain values and to demonstrate them through their actions as well as stated belief. For Jim, adopting this proper mode of conduct was also seen to give his children an appropriate social standing. It is impossible to know whether the parents of mixed heritage or mixed-race children feel this imperative more than other parents, but certainly all of the parents in this study were acutely aware of wanting their children to occupy a particular kind of place in the world. They knew this would not happen by accident. In other words, these parents knew or felt that their children would be 'out-of-place' to some degree or other and so theirs was a conscious effort to prepare their children for the future. Mavis and Doug, for example, chose to leave the USA to return to London so that their children would grow up in the right environment (less anti-Semitic, more diverse) and thus would more readily come to share the moral values to which they adhered. In their case they wanted a multi-cultural setting:

> **Mavis**: That was one of the reasons, I mean partly one of the reasons we wanted to move back was it was such a white America where we were living and we wanted to bring the kids back for a multi-racial upbringing as Doug had [had], to bring them back to London for that.

The tensions created by difference also created an awareness in the parents that their children had choices. The parents did not form a solid block through which they could assert that one culture, one religion, or even one set of family practices was either correct or 'normal'. While this may have once appeared like a cultural deficit, for these families it was treated more as a form of cultural capital:[7] the children could move across cultural boundaries while having sufficient cultural knowledge to make choices about how to conduct themselves and how they would want to identify themselves.

> **Interviewer**: So I mean how do you think your children would describe their cultural heritage?

Brigit: We – what is it they say? – they say Jewish-American-English-Caribbean-Black-White. They've sort of like got six different hyphens to their title. But we haven't actually – we can make an acronym of something you know and call them . . .

Henry: Yes. Mixed race, mixed religion, err mixed culture, yeah.

Brigit: He thinks it's kind of cool actually – they both do. They both think that they are quite unique and they are, you know.

Eleanor: Well [our son] describes himself as [. . .] mixture – he's half American and half British. He thinks of himself as Jewish. He doesn't think of himself as half Jewish and [half] Catholic – which I just find extraordinary. And he thinks of himself as entirely Scottish. Now for a kid who is really good at maths, you know [laughter] his fractions don't add up. So he has different cultural attachments depending on the purpose and how he happens to be feeling. So he, you know, he feels American. He has an American passport. He has an American birth certificate. He feels closer to his American-Jewish relatives than to the British ones partly because they have been warmer to him and more accepting of him.

Eleanor points to the way in which emotional attachment has been very important to the way in which her and Patrick's son became primarily self-identified as Jewish, but she also points to how his identifications might change. Moreover her reference to the fact that he is made up from too many 'halves' shows how, at an emotional level, there are no rigid boundaries to what can be absorbed and incorporated into a sense of self. For Henry and Brigit the whole point about bringing their children up in London rather than in New York or another big American city was that they would be freer to have multiple racial and other identities.

Henry: Yes they haven't had to choose what to be. Whether to choose to be White or to choose to be Black or to make or to have people put them in a cubby hole.

Brigit: Yeah impose their race and religion on them.

By comparison Mavis and Doug's sons did not actively identify as Jewish, although Mavis felt this to be part of a youthful rebellion

rather than a deep-seated rejection[8] (but who can tell?). And Helen
and Andrew's sons identified themselves as being Black British
rather than of mixed race mainly, she felt, because others saw them
that way due to their skin colour. This suggests that although these
young people of mixed heritage could make choices (not least
because of their class positions), they might find themselves in situations where other people or contexts might impose identities on
them rather than let these identifications be an outcome of 'free
choice' (if there is such a thing). Helen recognized that living in a
small, almost entirely white community, where the only ethnic mix
nearby was South Asian rather than Caribbean, meant that her sons
stood out in a crowd. In that sense they had less 'choice' about their
identifications than some of the other children being brought up in
larger mixed communities. Being of mixed heritage may have been
experienced as having less cachet for them in the public sphere,
although she did not feel that this was a problem for them in terms
of their own sense of security. Helen was ambivalent about some
aspects of heritage and neither she nor Andrew were interested in
going (back) to Jamaica, yet her family practices incorporated culturally diverse elements such as deliberately cooking in a West
Indian style; and they did give their daughter an African name.

> **Helen**: I don't [pause] I don't think personally that this issue of going
> back to the roots and the children knowing about their sort of her-
> itage and that point of view, I don't feel very strongly about that at
> all really. I see them as kind of Black British in a way. I wish I could
> see them as mixed-race British but that isn't how people perceive
> them because of how they look. And so I think that's what they are
> in a way. But I think it's just interesting for them to see where their
> parents came from; not really where they come from but where
> Andrew comes from and where their grandmum comes from. They
> laugh about certain little things that grandma does and so to me it's
> not a strong identity thing. I think the kids have got a really positive
> identity and they don't really need to know about Jamaica or Africa
> or all that business. I don't think that really figures that much.

Helen's account suggests that her children have established their
own identities, and although these incorporate threads of different

cultures and races, they are melded by their current context and family practices, rather than requiring a more substantial foundation deriving from knowledge of deeper ancestral roots such as those that might be traced to Africa. While we do not know what her children felt nor what they might come to feel, it is fairly clear from Helen and Andrew's accounts that in their slightly different ways they were engaged in a purposeful exercise of creating a desirable cultural context for their children, in which they could conduct themselves appropriately and from which they could derive and share the values of their families.

⋆ ⋆ ⋆

This chapter is essentially about the laying down of memories, the processes of creating bonds and bridges across generations, and the enfolding of new generations into webs of relationships that become part of a thoroughfare of emotions and values in everyday family life. I have relied upon stories collected from parents who have partnered across different cultural backgrounds because their awareness of difference and their desire to impart elements of different cultures and histories means that they did not take these practices for granted. These narratives have come from reflexive parents who are made more conscious of their practices through being to some degree out of place. In other words, few of them were living in their place of birth, while several had moved around a considerable amount before settling down. This experience of being out of place is also important because it renders the question of being 'at home' and having 'roots' more complex but also more visible. I have focused on largely positive accounts: the parents in this study have economic, social and cultural resources with which they can support their children. This means that issues of social class form an important context for the children of these parents. I am also conscious that these are parents whose strategies appear to have been successful, who have good relationships and who have deliberately nurtured the multi-cultural identities of their children. I have not dwelt on the negative aspects of being out of place (for example all these parents had experienced degrees of racism, anti-Semitism, or rejection not only by family members[9] but by society at large). This is not because I wish to present a rosy picture, but because my purpose has been to trace the ways in which parents use experiences and stories to give their children the knowledge and emotional resources to survive in a world in which they too will encounter (or already have encountered) similar things.

In creating a complex family tapestry into which children could be woven, it is particularly interesting to note that these parents – in the main – recognize that their children do not have fixed identities. They are depicted as rooted, yet fluid; bonded yet self-determining. This returns us to the apparent conflict of ideas outlined at the beginning of this chapter. There appear to be two dominant accounts about personal biographies: the first is the belief that secure roots and a known heritage are vital for ontological security; the second is the idea that we now make our own biographies and hence forge our life projects on the basis of choice (Beck and Beck-Gernsheim, 2002). This dichotomy leads to two more things. In the 'essential roots' narrative there is a presumption that there is something real located in the past, from which flows authenticity and real meaning. Here the past is reified and its role in providing ontological security is seen as automatic. In the 'choice' narrative the individual is seen to navigate his or her own meanings from a buffet of equally useful values, motifs and practices. In this version the past becomes a commodity rather than being a part of the self. Reflecting on the narratives of parents discussed here, we can see that neither of these versions captures the complexity and layers of the process of biography building. Some parents did provide accounts that could be seized upon as examples of a 'pick and mix' cultural affiliation (for example Brigit's children who have six components to their stated identities, the order of which could be rearranged). But it would be a very superficial reading of her story to put this kind of gloss on it. It would also ignore the work and resources that these parents put into providing a social context in which their children could feel 'free' to make their own choices. The parents had moved across the world, chosen a (relatively) safe place to live, selected specific schools and facilitated networks of family and friends to create the best environment for the children. They also tried to ensure that their children had the foundations for 'choice' drawn from their own biographies and identities. In other words, this is not an example of a moral or cultural free-for-all, nor could it happen in a vacuum. These children's biographies have elements of being self-made but mostly from fabrics woven by memory, emotion and context. I suggest we need to conceptualize these relational landscapes with greater attentiveness to personal resources. I do not mean by this what psychologists might call individual personality traits, nor do I simply mean economic resources and class power. Personal resources may include these elements, but I wish to denote a resource that is imbued with the cultural, the biographical, the historical and the spatial and can therefore be understood as not only fully social but sociological in its significance. It then becomes possible to look closely at how dimensions of class, gender and ethnicity work through these accounts, as well as how they are implicated in the context within which these stories are narrated. In this way it is also possible to attend to personhood and the complexities of real life, operating at a sociological level and not losing sight of nuance, difference and complexity.

5

Secrets and Lies

Uncovering family secrets has become a popular pastime. Not only do stories of revealed family secrets make good newspaper copy,[1] but genealogical searches are often tinged with the prospective excitement of finding a family secret buried in the past.[2] Stories of illegitimacy, bigamy and even criminality seem to have become charming – as long as they occurred sufficiently long ago. Part of the pleasure in uncovering secrets is perhaps the way in which the discovery gives the lie to the idea of an idyllic past, when families were all supposed to be respectable, god-fearing and law-abiding. It may also be that recognizing human frailty in the past helps us to be more understanding of contemporary failings and mistakes. Of course not all old secrets are at all charming: some retain their ability to scandalize or haunt in distressing ways,[3] so it would be unwise to assume that searching for secrets is always a harmless exercise. Notwithstanding the risks, however, it seem that the search for old secrets has become compelling and that the availability of census and other historical data on-line has fuelled the enthusiasm for this new pastime.

This fascination for old secrets is itself interesting: while the content of secrets (and the nature of things deemed shameful or unknowable) may change as social conditions change (Goudsblom and Mennell, eds, 1998; Davidoff et al., 1999), it seems that the desire to uncover past secrets is also subject to fluctuations and change. The contemporary thirst for 'truth' involves all manner of things but applies particularly to personal life. I start this chapter by outlining what I mean by this, since I do not see it as an inevitable nor even necessarily a good and enlightened process. I then turn to issues arising from the substance of certain family secrets and to give consideration to the sociological insights that secrets may provide in terms of changing class, gender and generational relationships.

The will to truth

Michel Foucault (1979, French orig. 1976) wrote extensively on what he termed 'the will to truth' as part of his analysis of the rise of scientific knowledge which developed a particular claim to truth which in turn asserted greater authenticity than other 'truths' (e.g. religion). Moreover, in terms of personal life, he identified the rise of the 'psy' professions (e.g. psychoanalysis, psychiatry and psychology) as crucial in the process of developing both supposedly fundamental knowledge about the self and different methodologies for excavating the authentic truth. He focused particularly on psychoanalysis as the talking cure through which individuals could be induced to tell everything about themselves to the analyst in order to find the source of all their personal problems. For Foucault the talking cure was the old Catholic confession re-vamped in a scientific form: he saw it as part of the modern governance of the self (both by the professions and by the individual) (Rose, 1991). This method, which became popularized throughout the twentieth century (e.g. through counselling and relationship manuals; see Giddens, 1992; Hazleden, 2004) came to insist that the healthy self and the healthy relationship requires truth-telling and also deep and intimate revelations about one's most authentic, but most hidden, core. This insistence on revelation in personal relationships has had parallel developments in other fields. So, for example, the solution to trauma came to be seen as revealing and retelling the harm done and the horror experienced in order to rid the incident of its

negative power. Memory work became very important in thera-
peutic encounters, particularly in relation to repressed experiences
and traumas such as child sexual abuse. And in Britain in the late
twentieth and early twenty-first centuries the professional response
even to such things as house-breaking or burglary is to offer a victim
support service, through which one can share and ultimately 'let go'
of the harmful feelings generated by this kind of personal invasion
(Furedi, 2004).

Much of the analysis done on the rise of disclosure of feelings
and emotions has focused on the difference between men and
women in their abilities and willingness to reveal their innermost
feelings and selves (Hazleden, 2004; Hochschild, 2003; Giddens,
1992). Men are typically depicted as resisting the call to disclose,
while women are seen as being on a determined mission to make
men reveal their true selves at very frequent intervals. These are
interesting themes, but I do not rehearse them here because I see
them as a diversion from the larger questions that the generalized
urge to discover and uncover secrets may show. Undoubtedly there
are differences of gender, generation, class, religion and ethnicity in
the felt urge to discover and reveal hidden truths (about either
oneself or one's family – or even nation), but to treat something like
the perceived differences between men and women as crucial leaves
untouched the idea that these identities are themselves discursively
and culturally constituted. These are not naturally given differences.
Those who resist, as much as those who yield to the compulsion to
disclose and discover, are equally subject to the overall directive that
there is something deeply meaningful and/or personal about secrets
and revelations. And while these events may be experienced in a
personal way, prioritizing the personal can overlook the social, historical, economic and cultural meaning of the ebb and flow of
secrets and disclosure over time. This leads me to suggest that it is
now timely to investigate family secrets (and other secrets for that
matter) in the same way that Norbert Elias investigated changing
manners and sensibilities in his *Civilizing Process* (2000, German
orig. 1939). Secrets are, of course, linked to sensibilities and to
shame which Elias wrote about extensively and so I lean heavily on
the general ideas he developed through painstaking historical analysis rather than embarking on a similar exercise. It is my intention to

pursue this theme through a particular family story/secret that I know well and this brings me on to a potentially controversial theme. I am using my own family history: I am now the sole keeper of the secrets and all the photographs, so I occupy a privileged position. Because all those who are involved in this story are dead and leave no direct or close descendants, my account cannot be challenged (although no doubt some family members, were they still living, could offer different recollections). The story revealed is one I have lived with for all my adult life and for that reason there are important methodological questions involved. This process involves the introduction of the autobiographical voice within the unfolding narrative and, as Arthur Bochner has argued, this is not always seen as acceptable within a sociological framework. As he states, using the personal voice:

> I believe the most devastating effect of these conventions is to establish and enforce a rule that we never allow our own experiences, feelings, or ideals to bias our scientific work. These conventions help us foster the illusion that our own relationships have little impact on our work: what we see, how we reflect on and interpret our results, what questions we ask, what answers we expect, and so on. They also help to sustain the myth that our research is divorced from our lives, that it has no autobiographical dimension, that what we do academically is not part of how we are working through the story of our own life. (2001: 138)

There is a particular irony too that, when one is a family researcher, it seems oddly inappropriate to acknowledge that one has personal relationships or even belongs to one's own family. Indeed the very idea that one might be interested in relationships because one has relationships oneself seems suspect – as if one is using work for one's own selfish purposes. Reference to the self is also sometimes seen as self-indulgent and even possibly slightly narcissistic. I am not sure if I can avoid all these criticisms except to argue that the story which unfolds below not only serves a sociological purpose but, I hope, also brings the issues into sharp focus by their very groundedness in real events. I situate the story in its historical era as it progressed and also make connections with broader structural factors, which go some of the way towards explaining the choices that were made. I also include some family photographs since the family album is such an important part of remembering these accounts (see chapter 2).

A case study of family secrets

In order to explore the social and cultural nature of secrets (and how they change over time) I now outline the progress of my family between approximately 1906 and 1976. The secrets which were fundamental to the family have certain aspects in common with moments experienced in history as it was played out in the south of England in the early to mid-twentieth century (Davidoff et al., 1999). But what is important about this story is the extent to which family secrets are revealed to be not simply something shameful, but active devices to be used and moulded for the sake of survival and self-improvement. The secret is not just something that is itself a passive thing which needs to be covered up, rather it has to be worked on and practised and geared to a particular goal or set of goals. I am suggesting that people actively work with their secrets, if only to hide them. They share them only carefully, and often only after the potential negative impact has expired. But at other times they are never revealed, and so there must be active work done to keep them secret and to ensure that subsequent generations do not find out. So this is the story of Gertrude and some of her daughters.

My grandmother Gertrude was born in 1882 at the height of the Victorian era. She was the youngest of eight children to be born into a poor rural family in Lincolnshire. At the time of the 1901 Census she was living with her widowed mother; both she and one of her older sisters had given birth to illegitimate children. They worked as domestics with the sister residing at the local manor house. Gertrude's future did not appear very bright but she was not without something of value, namely her good looks and ambition. She secured a marriage to a local sporting celebrity who was by comparison comfortably off and with a secure business and relatively well-heeled family background.

Plate 5.1 Gertrude in her prime

Of course in order to achieve this, her illegitimate daughter had had to be 'sent away' to relatives and it is quite possible that her husband never knew of the child. Gertrude went on to have four legitimate children but her marriage was not happy and there were suggestions of domestic violence. After the First World War her husband decided that the family should seek a better life in Australia

Plate 5.2 My maternal grandfather

and so took his eldest child, a son, and sailed away to set up home on the other side of the world before sending for his wife and three daughters. However, Gertrude had no intention of leaving England or of joining her husband. Staying put was the escape from her marriage that she wanted. Moreover, it was hard to imagine what postwar Australia would have to offer a young woman keen to put rural life and hardship behind her. But being left alone with three daughters (the youngest probably being only eight or nine years old) Gertrude was faced with a significant problem. Her in-laws would

Plate 5.3 My aunt (back row, third from the right) at a cabaret rehearsal, Paris 1932

not help her (as to them she was deserting her husband) and her own mother could not, so she took the course that many lone mothers were faced with at this time: around 1919 she put her children into an 'orphanage'. This was not only deeply shaming for the children, but (by report) a horrible experience. The sisters never saw their father again, and although their brother returned to England, they were estranged from him.[4] Meanwhile Gertrude went to London, where she found work in West End hotels and ultimately managed to buy a flat in a respectable part of town. One by one her daughters joined her as they reached an age when they could start working and earning. The middle daughter 'went on the stage' as a cabaret artiste and worked in London and Paris in the early 1930s. She married a wealthy older man who died within a short time and left her so well provided for that she never had to work again. The eldest daughter became a stenographer and worked in an elite organization until her brother-in-law bought her a small hotel which she ran with Gertrude until the 1970s. Both of these daughters spent their holidays on the French Riviera, dined in expensive hotels like the Ritz, bought jewellery and fur coats; mixing with – as they saw it – a very nice class of person. The third daughter disappointed them all by becoming a hairdresser and marrying 'down' (although sociologically speaking she married within her class).

From the 1930s to the 1970s the background of this family was safeguarded like a state secret, except that the illegitimate daughter (by this time respectably married) was reunited with her mother and half-sisters. Gertrude presented herself as a respectable widow with firm moral values[5] and together with her eldest daughter she became a member of the local Conservative Party and liked only to mix with 'well-to-do' folk. The family could not reveal its origins to the new circle of friends and acquaintances, not least because the period spent in the children's home carried the same sort of stigma as the Victorian workhouse. Had the truth been revealed, it was feared that they would be shunned for ever. Even in her nineties the eldest daughter absolutely refused to talk about her childhood or have it mentioned in her presence. The only one who did not feel so tightly bound by this secret, because she moved in very different circles, was the youngest daughter. She eventually told her own children, but not until after Gertrude's death.

Although this is a story of just one family it can be interrogated to reveal a great deal about issues of class, mobility, gender, sexuality and employment in the first half of the twentieth century in England. It is also a moral tale in the sense that we can see that the kinds of decisions taken were intentional and yet also heavily circumscribed by the place and time and overall milieu in which this family was operating. So although the moral choices made were personal, they also reflected the social conditions under which they were made. Consider the following aspects of social and cultural life at this time:

1   Gertrude was born poor and her father died before she was a year old. She became initially a domestic, living in a labourer's cottage with her mother, her illegitimate nephew and then her own illegitimate daughter. Her prospects were far from bright, but at the same time it was not particularly unusual for young rural women to have illegitimate children, nor was it rare for such children to be cared for by other relatives (Gill, 1977). Her

only chance of a better life was to 'marry up' and so she resorted to her only cultural (and embodied) capital, namely her physical attractiveness. Once again this was far from unusual: it had been featured in novels and other social commentaries for centuries (Hamilton, 1981, orig. 1909).

2 Gertrude's marriage was unhappy but at this time divorce was not a feasible option in law, and would in any case have been highly stigmatizing and prohibitively expensive (McGregor, 1957). If she was a victim of domestic violence it would have been ignored or treated as shameful and probably as her own fault (May, 1978). So her strategy of allowing her husband to emigrate with the false promise of joining him later was not unreasonable: at least outside the immediate family, this could leave her respectability intact (Klein, 2005).[6] Once the children were safely in the orphanage, she could move to a more anonymous city and pass herself off as a wife-in-waiting and later as a widow rather than a wife who had deserted her husband and then abandoned her children. Again Gertrude had few choices. It was impossible for her to keep the children with her. Stories from children's homes such as Barnardo's have since revealed that institutions like the one at which Gertrude left her daughters took in children whose parents could not look after them, or who were defined as destitute and not simply those who were orphans (Rose, 1987; and see http://www.bbc.co.uk/radio4/history/child_migrants.shtml).

3 Although Gertrude appeared to avoid disgrace and shame through this strategy, her daughters suffered beyond measure while they were in the home. They mixed with children from much more deprived backgrounds than themselves and so were bullied; they were also humiliated at school because they came from the children's home. Their futures must have looked bleak to them at that time, even if their mother's was in the ascendancy. The middle daughter (E) opted to run away but then had to take the only career path available to 'independent' young women without office skills in the 1920s. She joined the chorus line, knowing that it was tinged with potential disgrace. But this was the 'Flapper Era', so the risqué was also acceptable on the fringes of what was known as 'Society' (i.e. the smart London set). The

Plate 5.4 Society wedding

family was clearly walking a tightrope at the time. Show business
was not respectable, but it was glamorous and it offered a more
exciting life than many other options open to young women.
Since this work was likely to be short-lived, beneath it lay a much
more important strategy, namely marriage to the kind of wealthy
man who would enjoy night life and cabarets.

E was, of course, denounced as a 'gold digger' and moral repro-
bate by her husband's first family but it is important to consider
her 'choices' at that time. From the point of view of the secure and
moneyed middle class from which her husband came, the marriage represented a disreputable step and also a potential depletion
of the family's asset, since his sons by his first marriage had the rea-
sonable expectation of inheriting the family business and its
wealth on the death of their father. But from the point of view of
those aspiring to join the respectable middle class, the marriage
was ideal, especially as E's cultural capital was waning as she aged.
In terms of gender politics her husband was in a very powerful
position but this also meant that it was vital for E's family to present
themselves as being as respectable as possible. It was imperative that
the family's secrets did not leak out, since the whole family was
likely to benefit from the marriage. The marriage, and then the
early death of E's husband, meant that economic and cultural
resources did flow into the family. Gertrude did not have to worry
about an impoverished old age, and the two older sisters acquired
their much needed nest-eggs to see them through to old age.[7]

4   These kinds of alliances and economic exchanges between
    families were fairly common, but bridging the considerable
    difference in family background for E and her husband would
    have been facilitated by social conditions during the Second
    World War when they married. Sexual risk-taking became less
    unusual, and there was also a sense in which the old order –
    signified by the elaborate class differences of the 1930s –
    was beginning to break down (Marwick, 1971, 1982; *Royal
    Commission on Marriage and Divorce, 1951–5*, 1956). E's life
    chances were therefore influenced by a number of overlapping
    factors, from a growing recognition that single women had to
    work for a living, that values about class and sexuality were
    changing, that mobility from country to town was becoming
    easier, and that glamour had a social cachet which could obscure
    class background (to some extent). Living in London from the
    mid-1920s, throughout the war and thereafter, was also an
    essential element in the changes that she achieved. Moreover, E
    and her older sister B were avid readers of etiquette books and

availed themselves of the necessary cultural paraphernalia of upward mobility from ivory cigarette holders from Harrods to Art Deco furniture from Heal's (Bowlby, 2001). Indeed the ability to negotiate fashionable department stores, hotels and restaurants was vital. B even changed the name by which she was known, Florence, considered to be rather dull, Victorian and potentially lower class, to a nickname with distinctly P. G. Wodehouse overtones, which she found racy, fashionable and fun.[8] All of these changes took skill, vigilance and determination as the family (or most of it) was attempting to remould itself completely. They worked on changing their sensibilities and acquiring cultural capital in a way that might have astounded Elias, who saw such changes occurring over decades and centuries rather than within a generation.

This is far from being a unique story of social mobility (Kuhn, 1995; Steedman, 1986); indeed we could argue that the story (with its successes, failures and secrets) is itself a modern stylized narrative rather than an innocent recounting of factual events. These stories are themselves now quite fashionable.[9] The ebb and flow of generations of families, and especially their secrets which can either 'make' or 'undo' them, seem to be fascinating. In sociological terms, however, their importance lies in understanding how such events as the birth of an illegitimate child or a marriage breakdown should be a necessary social secret at one period of history, later to become absorbed and accepted as an ordinary life event. Elias's concept of figuration is helpful here as it requires us to envisage all the overlapping elements of social, cultural and economic life of a given historical moment and to see how shifts in some fields iterate with shifts elsewhere to produce certain types of outcome which in turn influence a part of yet another field and so on. Moreover, his insistence that this occurs within the framework of time passing such that nothing actually stays the same means we have to be attentive to social and historical time as well. This means that it is often easier to see how families created the image that they desired of themselves in the past than it is to see this process happening in the present. It is harder to see these fabrications as they unfold because they are the actualities into which we are born, and misinformation and misrepresentations become part of each new generation's reality and memory (see chapter 4). Take these quotations, for example, from a grandfather and grandmother interviewed in 2001 as part of a project on kinship after divorce:[10]

> **Reg** [aged seventy-eight]: Yes, yes my family was a Victorian family and my father was the younger one of the family but yes I don't remember any divorces. There was only one, I had a cousin who had a – I don't know if it was illegitimate or not, I don't know much of the background, anyway she's still living, this cousin. But that lad was born just after the war. Well [it was] something [to do] with movement of people in the war. My cousin who was, I think, she was a cook or chef or something in the service; I think it's there where it happened. But I don't know anything about it, I wasn't told anything and I thought it wasn't anything to do with me, so really all my aunts and uncles, yes they all married.

> **Emily** [aged sixty-six]: Well personally speaking I would think [my values come] from my parents [. . .], because again they were a lovely couple, we were a close family at home; grandparents were always close to us so probably the foundation is there really isn't it, you know I've not had any experience of any, what shall we say, family falling out or anything like that so that's probably where it is. If I say to you that I know it might be strange but you might be interested, when my father died and we had the funeral, I can always remember the minister saying in our house, that he had never met such a close family which is a lovely thing to say really, I mean alright we're brothers and sisters [and have had] fall-outs, ups and downs and what have you. That in a nutshell is it for me you know with being a close family and I just like to think that we're all a very close family as well I think we are very supportive of each other.

Reg here makes it clear that there was something 'unorthodox' in his wider family but 'he was never told anything' and obviously he was not sufficiently interested to find out. So he could present his family as 'Victorian', which meant presumably properly patriarchal, with no sex before marriage, illegitimacy, adultery or any other misdemeanour. From this baseline Reg was able to compare contemporary families in order to find them lacking the moral fibre and appropriate codes of behaviour found in the past. Emily also depicts her family in idealized terms, but what is impossible to know is whether her view was constructed as ideal through the banishment of those who did not fit in some way or whether her family was unusually fortunate in being able to conform to the immediate pre- and post-war ideal. Thus during this time (c.1925–50) children generally knew nothing about exiled uncles or aunts or female cousins who disappeared briefly to nursing homes in the country to give birth and have their illegitimate children adopted secretly (Spensky, 1992). The fiction may have been their lived reality, against which modern behaviour can be (unsurprisingly) judged rather harshly. Often people we interviewed appeared to have suspicions that all might not have been as idyllic as they had been led to believe, but either they never had the chance to pursue their suspicions or they did not wish to upset surviving relatives by raising issues long put to rest. For some, of course, secrets are now being revealed as letters from charities and other organizations who help illegitimate, adopted or foundling children find their blood relatives drop unexpectedly through the letter box. The contemporary desire to find the apparent truth of one's origins and identity means that some old secrets are coming to light and there is a growing sense that secrets formed today may be less 'safe' and more vulnerable to disclosure than those forged by our grandparents' generation.

Modern secrets

Although the climate of most of the first half of the twentieth century in Britain largely favoured keeping family 'irregularities' private, this preference has to some extent been reversed. I now trace this shift by exploring paternity, to see how values about truth, secrecy and lies have changed radically and how the demise of this particularly rich area of secrecy is impacting upon relationships within families and kin. While it was once entirely normative to treat paternity as a matter of pragmatics rather than biological truth, it is now almost impossible to keep secrets about biological paternity; those who seek to do so are increasingly identified as being outside appropriate moral boundaries.

English common law has long been party to a certain amount of deceit about paternity – albeit often in the interests of the welfare of children. For example there has long existed a presumption of legitimacy through which it was maintained that a child born to a married woman was the legal child of her husband (Smart, 1987). Although this presumption was rebuttable there has been extensive case law (notably since the *Banbury Peerage Case* in 1811) that documents stringently the conditions under which such rebuttals could take place. This was mainly because the effect of bastardizing a child could be devastating both socially and economically. Such a child would not be supported by any father, could no longer inherit and would no longer be treated as a relative of his or her half-siblings. The 'fatherless' child would be cast into a legal limbo. Until methods of scientific testing of paternity started to be developed, a husband could not bastardize a child of his wife's if there was any evidence, on the balance of probabilities, that he could have had intercourse with her at the relevant time (assuming of course that he was not infertile or impotent). This would tend to mean that if a woman was having a sexual relationship with another man at around the same time as with her husband, it would be very hard for him to prove in law that he was not the father. In any case, legal procedures tended to be the preserve of the wealthy and propertied, so it would be unlikely for most of the fathers who had doubts about paternity to be in a position to do anything decisive about it.

The presumption of legitimacy is rarely invoked now because of the possibility of genetic testing, which can usually prove the identity of a child's father beyond doubt. But the rise of earlier forms of medical technology in the twentieth century did not automatically lead to the supremacy of biological truth in matters of paternity. For example, it was common in the early days of artificial (now assisted) insemination by donor for the mother's husband to enter his name on the child's birth certificate as the father. The medical profession colluded in this practice until it was made lawful for husbands to register their legal paternity legitimately after the introduction of the 1990 Human Fertilization and Embryology Act (Jackson, 2001). In the 1950s it was felt to be in the child's best interests for the husband simply to claim paternity[11] and to act as the child's natural father so that the family could present itself as a 'normal' family. Infertile husbands were also spared having their shame known by family and friends; male infertility was often safeguarded as yet another family secret. The parents of children born through artificial insemination by donor (AID) were also actively discouraged from telling their offspring about the nature of their conception and their actual genesis (Smart, 1987). Thus it would have come as a considerable shock to many adults in the 1980s or 1990s to discover that their fathers were not their biological progenitors.

Even as late as the 1990s the English courts were making decisions about paternity disputes which meant that children could not undergo blood tests unless mothers were willing to expose their children to the possible knowledge that the man they thought was their father (typically the mother's husband) was in fact a biological stranger. Jane Fortin (1994) has described this as the 'Gooseberry Bush Approach'. Her discussion of the court's approach was based on the case of *Re F* which went to court in 1992 with a little girl (E) of thirteen months as the focus of a paternity dispute.[12] Mrs F was having an affair at the time of E's conception, but by the time she was born the affair was ended and E was being brought up as Mr F's daughter with his full knowledge of the situation. At the time of this case DNA testing made the results of blood tests much more reliable than they had been in previous decades, when they did little more than point to a likelihood of a given man's paternity. None the less, the courts preferred to leave the identity of the child's father in doubt because they could see no benefit in disrupting the family or of giving the other man a potential link with the child. This case was controversial because in earlier instances the courts had ordered blood tests to be taken. However, as Fortin points out, these were cases when married men were disputing paternity – in other words they were refusing to accept that children born to their wives were their own. In the case of *Re F*, the husband wanted the child to be treated as his own, he was not trying to disown her, and so the court's decision allowed this married nuclear family to sustain the pretence that they were all 'properly' biologically related.

Fortin's criticism of the judgement in this case is interesting because she suggests that the court did not give enough weight to the child's right to know her correct parentage and genetic inheritance. But Fortin does not see this simply as a legal right which should have carried influence, she sees it as a psychological need which is also part of the safeguarding of the child's future welfare. In this argument Fortin demonstrates clearly how ideas about secrets over paternity changed over the course of the twentieth century. She depicts the judges as outmoded in their thinking, too closely committed to preserving a particular type of family arrangement rather than seeing the importance of accurate knowledge of the scientifically verified truth of conception. She states:

> When the child's need for knowledge of origins is eventually recognised as being separate from his need for social parenthood, the decision in *Re F* may come to be viewed simply as a Luddite refusal to face up to the implications of DNA profiling and such a 'gooseberry bush approach' as unnecessary paternalism. (1994: 307)

Fortin appears to be unwavering in her certainty that scientifically based knowledge/truth is best. Earlier generations in analogous instances were just as certain that a child's welfare would be best protected if she was raised in ignorance. It was felt that children would settle best in a family where the head of household believed himself to be the biological father and where all the children also believed that their social father was their biological father. Indeed, it is not entirely clear that the judges were altogether out of step with the way in which 'ordinary' families operated and perhaps still operate. In a study of paternity secrets, Lyn Turney interviewed fifteen women who had experience of 'paternity uncertainty'. Typically these women were in a long-term relationship or were married, but had had affairs or one-night stands so that they were not sure who had fathered their children. Turney argues that at the time of her study in Australia, women who 'deceived' their partners into believing that the children they were raising were their genetic offspring were vilified both because they were passing off another man's child on an innocent partner, but also because they were depriving their child of the right to know his or her true parentage. However, from the interviews she discovered that the situation in which the women found themselves was much more complicated than this. Many feared that their existing partner would leave them if the other sexual liaison were revealed, and that the upheaval would be harmful for the child they were carrying. Others feared violence and so were simply too afraid to rock the boat. None wanted to find a solution through abortion since they felt that there was a strong chance that the child had been fathered by the live-in partner and they wanted to give birth to and raise the infant. As Turney argues:

> From the presented accounts, it is clear that paternity secrets are deeply held, complex, and difficult to disclose. Failing to immediately confess another, and often unimportant, distasteful or distressing sexual event, in the context of an unexpected pregnancy and a promising or permanent relationship, set these women on a trajectory from which it became increasingly difficult to exit. [. . .] The imperative to tell the truth was weighed against the harsh moral judgments that attend the moral panic about them. (2005: 243)

In other words, Turney's research reveals the extent to which the personal and social conditions under which these women were living made it hard for them to tell the possible truth about the paternity of the child they were carrying. Although the cultural context was changing (viz. the trend towards scientifically based truths about paternity combined with a child's legal right to know), social conditions for many of these women proved incongruous with the new, stringent requirements. While women who deceive their husbands about paternity have long been vilified (*Royal Commission on Marriage and Divorce, 1951–55,* 1956), there was in the past at least a countervailing imperative to safeguard children by not bastardizing them and by seeking to raise them in a 'normal' family. In the contemporary situation there is no longer a cultural counter-balance and the woman who deceives is seen to harm her child as well as her partner. Ironically, this vilification tends to be counter-productive, in that some contemporary mothers feel compelled to keep any secret about paternity to themselves for as long as possible.

There are also competing gender agendas in relation to paternity secrets. Fathers have become increasingly interested in establishing paternity,[13] not least because proof of non-paternity provides relief from child-support payments, but equally because it may lead to peace of mind where there had been doubt. Mothers may be less enthusiastic about DNA testing because of the fear of rejection of both the child and of themselves. The Child Support Agency in the UK requires that mothers applying for social security must provide the name of the child's father (or receive lower benefit levels); this means that a man with whom the mother does not wish to continue any relationship can, once paternity is established, acquire parental responsibility for the child as well as demanding contact. Mothers are therefore increasingly finding they cannot keep these secrets and that strategies and/or solutions once available are diminishing.

The modern cultural distaste for secrets applies also to cases of adoption, where adoptive parents are increasingly required to be open about a child's origins (Smith and Logan, 2004), and to the process of assisted reproduction, where sperm donors in the UK no longer have the option of anonymity (Donovan, 2006). It is now argued that there is no intrinsic harm for children to know from an early age that they have both biological and social parents; there is no need for the secrecy of the past as there is no longer any shame or disgrace in having more than two parents or sets of parents. Where there are any difficulties, it is argued, it is possible to compensate for them by achieving certain knowledge of one's identity and ontological security; in the process one might also gain an understanding of any diseases and genetic conditions that may have been inherited. Yet as Turney's research has indicated, some people may still feel the need to keep secrets and research on people's attitudes to genetic testing also suggests that not everyone is willing to share knowledge about inherited conditions, even with kin who may be directly affected by the same condition or disease. Alison Shaw's (forthcoming) discussion of South Asian families and genetic testing, for example, has shown that people may feel it is unethical to 'worry' their kin about a disease they may not get or which may not ultimately be passed on. Thus the status of scientific knowledge, and even the right to know, can be subject to codes of familial relationships that may apply different ethical criteria. Secrets may be felt to be necessary for the preservation of relationships and the 'truth' may be taken to be less important than stabilizing fictions.

The recent history of the legal status of paternity in Britain is not a simple story of the triumph of knowledge over ignorance, nor of truth over lies and certainty over doubt. Rather it reveals a complex tapestry of concerns over changing levels of stigma and shame, changing legal rights, changing gender relationships, changing relationships across generations, changing technologies, changing concepts of welfare and so on. It is not a matter of whether it is better to keep secrets or better to know/tell the truth: it is important to note how people manage both secrets and truths at different moments and in different conditions. The mother who refuses a blood test on her child, because it may show that the man she had an affair with is the biological father of her child, may now appear monstrous. But in 1992 Judge Callman (in *Re F* above) found that just such a mother was entirely right to refuse a blood test; he supported her (and her husband) in bringing up the child as 'theirs', without involving a potential but extraneous biological father in the child's life. He felt it was best not to disrupt the family. His judgement would not be able to stand a decade later, but this reveals only how cultural conditions change; it does not mean that he was wrong, nor does it mean that the mother was a bad or deceitful parent. The case shows how, in the course of just a decade, an apparently sensible and caring course of action can be redefined as a harmful subterfuge likely to damage a child emotionally and psychologically. Thus the changing status of secrets reflects a complex change in the normative and cultural order. But it also impacts upon personal relationships.

★   ★   ★

It is difficult to predict how the insistence on genetic truths or even on intimate revelations such as 'admitting' being a sperm or egg donor to a new partner will change personal relationships. But as far as genetic truths are concerned it is clear that both law and family policies have shifted to accommodate the new trend with remarkable speed (Freeman and Richards, 2006). Adoptive parents are now encouraged to view adoption as a way of looking after someone else's child rather than acquiring their 'own' child. And there is a clear policy preference for allowing an adopted child to know about their bio-parent(s) and even to have contact if it is suitable and feasible. In such cases children clearly have more than two parents and the place of the social parent is acknowledged alongside the biological parent. Equally, after divorce in most Western societies, children are encouraged to remain in contact with their biological fathers and, where possible, to live with both parents, thus creating a situation where the child may have sets of bio-parents and step in different households (Smart et al., 2001). Moreover, the practice in the UK whereby a new step-parent could adopt his wife's child by a previous marriage (thus legally excluding a biological parent) has now fallen out of favour because the pretence of being a nuclear family, which was once thought to be vital to a child's welfare, has given way to the idea that maintaining contact with all biological parents is the best policy. So the idea of multiple parents is now fairly common: it has become possible for many adults who have been involved in a child's life to apply for 'parental responsibility' orders, which gives them a say in the child's upbringing as well as the possibility of long-term contact. What is more, as Sally Sheldon (2005) has argued, fatherhood in particular is changing dramatically. She discusses the case of *In Re D* in which an unmarried couple began a course of IVF treatment together, arising from the man's infertility.[14] After one cycle of treatment the woman failed to conceive and the couple split up. But the woman returned to the clinic for another cycle of treatment and became pregnant. The daughter she gave birth to had no genetic relationship to her former partner, but he (Mr B) applied to be acknowledged as the child's legal father and to have contact with the baby. By this time, the mother had repartnered and did not want her former partner to be a 'parent' to the child: they no longer had a relationship and the child was not 'his'. Ultimately (after the case went to the Court of Appeal) Mr B was not granted legal paternity, although the first judge in a lower court had decided in his favour. He was, however, allowed to have indirect contact with the child. Although the case did not unreservedly recognize that he should be seen as the legal father to this child, the considerations followed in the case at appeal show how far legal policy has shifted such that he was almost successful. Sheldon notes:

> The legal response to the facts of *In Re D* is a flexible one which accords specific rights on the basis of a child's perceived best interests. Within

this vision, the fact that a man is named on a birth certificate is seen as less important than giving him some role in a child's life as a provider of information and as a possible future social father. Further, the case recognises that the presence of one man in the mother's life is not a bar to some limited participation by another. However, *In Re D* recognises a man who has no genetic links with a child, no existing social relationship with her, and no ongoing relationship with her mother as having paternal rights and interests which merit legal protection. (2005: 360)

Sheldon poses the question of what impact this will have on this child's family unit, since Mr B can contact the child and tell her of the part he played in her conception; he may also progress to having actual contact with her. The child's birth mother does not have the option of keeping the facts of IVF conception from the child; furthermore, she cannot pretend to the child that her current partner – whom the child may think of as her father – is her biological father. While it may be 'a good thing' that the child cannot be deceived in this way, it does mean that the mother is obliged to accommodate Mr B into her daughter's life even though he is neither 'kin' nor even a friend. The shape of her family life will be influenced by this. By extension from this case, it is possible to see how other families might similarly take on different shapes to those that might have been expected. The boundaries of 'the family' will necessarily become more fluid as more people are accommodated within the remit. It may also be that some relationships founder as a consequence. In this case it is clear that the Court of Appeal was worried that the mother's new relationship might not survive if Mr B became the acknowledged legal father of the child; this was seen as potentially harmful to the child because her home life would become less stable and secure. In other words, it was not only the mother and daughter who would have to accommodate Mr B, but also the mother's new partner, and he might not be either willing or compliant.

There is therefore a possible incongruence between what is seen to be a progressive policy based on genetic truths and/or the recognition that several people may have a legitimate interest in a child, and the way in which many couples think that family life should be ordered and lived. The end of secrecy (or at least this kind of secret) appears to be bringing with it multiple parents (or adults in parental roles); this means that relationships are created not only between the child and each adult, but also between and across all the adults involved. These relationships may be superficial as far as the adults are concerned, but in as much as they matter to the child for whom each adult cares, they cannot be easily dismissed, demeaned or ignored. This is therefore likely to create a very different landscape for many families and even to change the cultural imaginary of what a family should look like. Perhaps the idealized nuclear family of the past could survive only on the basis of its many and varied family secrets; rather than undermine that familial structure, it is possible that such secrets were its very supports. The need for a certain kind of secrecy (as in the case of my grandmother in the 1920s or in that of Mrs F in 1992) was a response to social vulnerability: the secrets served as a form of protection against hardship or rejection. But the insistence on 'truth' and transparency now creates other forms of vulnerability, especially in cases where social mores have not changed greatly. The availability of scientific certainty about paternity can cut across delicate social relationships, but it can also create networks of fictive kin that arise in spite of people's wishes, not necessarily through choice. Ironically, just as research is focusing on families of choice and the centrality of negotiations in relationships, new kinds of compulsory relationships are being forged. Alongside this potential realignment, it is important to remember the extent to which these are also relationships of power. The drive to truth (as for example in Fortin's argument) presumes that openness will create an equality of knowledge among people who then become equally positioned in relation to each other. However, the parties themselves may not be on an equal footing, so this kind of openness may bring with it forms of vulnerability as well as different forms of regulation of personal life. In making this point I am not arguing that secrets are 'good things', nor that it was better when the nuclear family sustained its apparent reputation by keeping secrets; rather I am suggesting that changing the rules, whether about which secrets to keep or which to reveal, does not transform relations of power between classes, genders and generations. These new truths are simply played out on the existing social landscapes. This inevitably brings me on to further consideration of the downside of personal life and intimacy. In the next chapter I explore what it means to experience powerlessness in relationships and to endure poor or harmful attachments.

6

Families we Live with

In this chapter I turn attention towards some of the everyday issues that are faced in the living of family life, or as David Morgan would say, in family practices. I focus on the difficulties of sustaining relationships with kin and family members and how feelings such as dislike and distress have to be managed. The centrality of emotions to an understanding of families and relationships is discussed in chapter 3 above, but there my focus turned to issues of love and commitment, emphasizing positive emotions and the good or 'magical' qualities of love. I now explore darker themes because these too are often overlooked in sociological literature, except in relation to families or relationships breaking down, the hardship and problems surrounding unemployment and poverty (Allan, 1985) or feminist work on domestic violence. Although I pursue some aspects of relationship breakdown here, I am more concerned to examine the experiences of living in and with on-going difficult relationships and the extent to which any relationship can ebb and flow as people grow or as circumstances and contexts change. The popular insistence on good-quality relationships, combined with the casual presumption that there are quick and easy exits from poor relationships, can create an impression that difficulties can be overcome by moving on. The individualization thesis has contributed to this by seeming to suggest that individuals can simply walk away from unsatisfactory relationships, giving rise to the idea that people are no longer prepared to endure or work through negative relationships.

Possibly at odds with the idea of the easy exit is the voluminous popular literature on relationship management and self-help manuals intended to offer advice on improving relationships. This, combined with the growth in reality television programmes such as *Supernanny*, *The Teen Tamer*, *Brat Camp* and even one-offs such as Ursula Macfarlane's documentary about divorce, *Breaking up with the Jones* (2006), suggests that many people are enduring less than perfect relationships with their spouses, partners, children, parents, sibling and other relatives and are seeking to find solutions. As Ian Craib has argued:

> If we take seriously [. . .] that the biological necessities of reproduction entail that men and women must both love and hate each other, then the guides for the 'pure relationship' attempt to suppress the dynamics that result from this. Jealousy, possessiveness, devotion, sacrifice, rage, brutality, respect, tenderness, understanding all have their part to play. (1994: 178)

Craib comes to his conclusions through psychoanalytic thinking. While in this book I am striving to discover what a sociological perspective can offer, I find that among Craib's strengths is his recognition that the dark sides of relationships cannot be eliminated easily – or perhaps at all. I am less convinced than Craib that people must hate each other if they are also to love each other, so I do not endorse the idea of an eternal antipathy as the human condition. However, Craib does bring these issues into the light and insists that we do not imagine that they are easily overcome. He is some-what scathing of Giddens (1992), whom he sees as 'employing anodyne notions of respect, equality and so on' (1994: 178) to achieve/promote 'pure relationships'; in Craib's view, our negative feelings are so deeply rooted that mere adherence to a new cultural etiquette of personal relationships hardly touches the surface of our more difficult emotions. Such criticism might founder when one thinks about how sensibilities can change over time or in relation to changing mores as opposed to changes in fundamental human psychology. But Craib's emphasis on dark emotions does reveal the tenacity of such feelings; it also throws some light on why such values as equality, respect and dignity may find their least purchase in families and close personal relationships, even when those values may be taken for granted in the work place and elsewhere outside the home.

The quoted passage from Craib prioritizes heterosexual, adult couple relationships, but he does not ignore other relationships; neither does he exclude one's negative relationship with oneself. While adult (heterosexual) couple relationships are clearly important, he acknowledges that they may not be the most important, and that they certainly change in importance over the life course. So everyday negative feelings in relationships, whether or not they are an ontological given, flow in many directions. This might have particular salience for children, not simply because children tend to have less understanding of negative emotions and fewer experiences to help deal with them, but because dependent children cannot escape from difficult relationships with parents and/or with siblings (Mitchell, 2003). So there are certainly no quick escapes for children, even if there are *some* escape routes for adults. But arguments I have put forward in previous chapters also suggest that while a physical escape from relationships may be possible for adults, other elements of these relationships may be slow to relinquish their grip. For example, couples may separate from one another but if they are parents they may remain linked through their children. Moreover, the contemporary policy emphasis on continuing to share parenting after separation means that the parents often have to manage some kind of contact with each other, even if they no longer live in the same household (Smart and Neale, 1999). It is also naïve to imagine that relationships (or at least the consequences and memories of relationships) end just because people cease to live together or cease to have much contact with each other. So poor relationships are a part of family life and family members just have to live with them:

Interviewer: What's it like living in your family?
Pete [aged six]: Horrible.
Interviewer: Can you tell me why?

Pete: Because people smack people. . . .

Interviewer: Are there any things you'd like to change about your family?

Pete: That we could have got on better.

This exchange comes from one of our studies on children's experiences of post-divorce family life.[1] Pete, who lived with his father and was only six years old at the time of the interview (conducted with his older brother, who had speech problems), is explaining in straightforward terms why his family does not make him happy; he also spoke of episodes of considerable violence and harmful neglect visited on the boys by their non-residential mother's new husband. Parents' violence towards their children and towards each other occasionally featured significantly in the accounts we collected from children, reflecting distressingly deteriorated relationships. While Pete and his brother came from a deprived family background, we found equally impoverished relationships in relatively affluent surroundings:

> **Adrian** [aged 15]: [My dad] and mum used to still have arguments because when she'd left, she still used to baby-sit us. We had arguments and it ended up once she turned round and she hit me, and I said 'I'm not going to take this from you' and I turned round and belted her back. And me dad sided with me, not my mum. Me dad actually lashed [out] at me once 'cause he forced me to the carpet, and it ended up him kicking me, and mum said 'Now, you've had enough.' And dad turned round and swept her feet from underneath her, and she ended up falling and all these biscuits went flying everywhere. And I said 'Thank you very much' and laughed. That was when she were baby-sitting, my dad was sat in the room for a minute before he went out, and he were just laughing.

We interviewed Adrian's sister separately. She confirmed the degree of violence in the household, including the fact that Adrian had started to 'beat her up' too. What is more, in some families, aunts, uncles and grandparents could all become involved in family rows, fights and arguments.

Children from these kinds of households could often hardly wait to leave home. Until they reached an appropriate age, went to university or formed a relationship, however, they tended to feel trapped. Adrian's sister was attempting to go to a solicitor to have the residence order that had been established on her parents' divorce changed so that she could live with her mother. But she was too frightened to raise the issue with her father, and her mother was, it appears, also incredibly worried about upsetting him. These stories reveal the powerlessness of children, who can do no more than wait until it becomes possible to leave. Unfortunately for the younger ones this exit could seem a very long way away.

So, in this chapter I explore the problems of being embedded in a family or in relationships that cannot easily be escaped. Embeddedness and connectedness are therefore not to be taken as *a priori* good things. While I do not ignore the significance of physical violence, I do not dwell on this subject because such manifestations of power and negativity have been fairly well explored in domestic violence literature (e.g. Edwards, 1989; Hester, 2000; Webster, 2002; Hanmer et al., 1999). Rather I concentrate on less visible and possibly less dramatic instances of everyday unhappiness in order to flesh out the imperfections of the 'families we live with' and to counter the idea that in late modern society the individualized actor can always maximize personal happiness. It is also necessary to provide a corrective to the contemporary idealization of family life: while it is of course possible to recognize how important families and intimacy usually are, this very importance may lie in their potentially damaging and harmful qualities. My themes are the everyday experiences of anxiety, hurt and lack of respect. But I must start with a word of caution. As Janet Finch and Jennifer Mason have pointed out, people are often reluctant to talk to outsiders about bad relationships or to admit that they do not like some of their close kin. For example, in their study of kinship obligations Finch and Mason discuss the case of 'Jane Jones' who, in the context of borrowing and lending money, implies that one of her sons had certain undesirable qualities; however, she is cautious about doing so. Finch and Mason argue:

> What is striking is that neither she − nor any other parent − *portrays herself* as disliking a child. This in itself reinforces our point about demeanour. There is a sense in which for a parent (perhaps particularly

a mother) to show that her overall feeling is dislike would reflect badly upon herself, as the person who brought up that child. (1993: 130; emphasis in original)

This implies that it is often quite hard to get at the kinds of negative feelings that people may have for one another in the course of most research on on-going family life. While negative expressions about former spouses or partners are common after separation, and perhaps siblings may be willing to be critical of each other, it is usually difficult to tap into negative feelings between people whose relationships are on-going. Penny Mansfield and Jean Collard (1988) found that the newly wed couples they interviewed would temper their disappointment in each other by reducing the seriousness of the problem or the significance of the issue at hand. What is more, in our research on children in post-divorce families we found that children were extremely cautious about expressing criticism of their parents (Smart et al., 2001). It was often not until we returned to interview the children a second time (four years later[2]) that many ventured some criticism, while very few suggested that they did not like one or other of their parents, if not both and/or any of the other adults involved. So it is not easy to appreciate some of the actualities of everyday family life. Seeking to do so can raise a number of problematic ethical issues. For example, the six-year-old Pete (quoted above) was very candid, but it is also possible that he 'gave away' more than he might have wanted to on reflection. Other children too might have unintentionally revealed certain insights into their families. It was clear in some instances that children felt it would be disloyal to say what they really felt about a situation, or to explain fully what was going on.[3] But equally we found that as they got older (and arguably more aware of the significance of an interview), children could become more open – although even then within limits. So it is important to consider how such data should be handled and interpreted; furthermore, it may be that interviewees should be given the opportunity to take back or re-phrase some of the things they say.[4] But this assumes that interviews press people into saying more than they want to. Our experience, however, was often that people, especially children, were pleased to have an opportunity to give their views and to explain personal matters from their own point of view. Moreover, avoiding difficult issues can involve the risk of sociological accounts of family life becoming unable to represent the full diversity of relationships and emotions, presenting only an anodyne, one-dimensional, cuddly version of couple or intergenerational relationships. As always, ethics in research are a matter of balance, so the scenarios presented below are intended to present the complexities of family living, and should not be read as any kind of deliberate criticism of the people involved. I now turn to some of the key themes involved in problematic, on-going relationships.

Living with anxiety

I take anxiety to mean an emotional response to significant personal difficulties, often involving conflicting duties or responsibilities which can give rise to a sense of powerlessness and an inability to know what to do about the worries that beset one. Andrew Sayer has written about a range of emotions in connection with his arguments about the connections between emotion and morality, which in turn is linked to one's social class position and/or the operations of class in British society. He focuses on benevolence, compassion, envy, justice, toleration, shame and humiliation and points to the ways in which these feelings reveal a normative order that is closely associated with class inequalities. For example, shame may be experienced by a man whose wife goes out to work even though, objectively speaking, this is far from a shameful act. Sayer points out that the shame is embedded in a social understanding that working-class men *should* be able to provide for their families (in spite of class disadvantages): the strong feelings of shame can be understood only if we appreciate the social constructions of both gender and class at specific moments in history. The emotion therefore tells us about the society or community inhabited by the specific actors, as well as the extent to which values are internalized and treated as personal. Through his various examples of emotions that are linked to moral positions, Sayer transcends the ubiquitous divide between the personal and the public (i.e. by revealing the sociological context of feelings) but he also brings the personal dimension of feelings directly into sociological focus by showing the complexities of how class works on a daily, emotional level. In other words, he suggests that sociology fails to understand class if it cannot also bring these emotions/moralities into focus.

In the areas of gender and generation I suggest that we can do similar work (i.e. bring emotions into sociological focus) by looking at some of the expressed negative or painful emotions that tell us not only about the individual, but about the way in which all individuals position themselves in the context of their daily lives. As Sayer argues:

> I have emphasised how moral and immoral sentiments relate to class, but [. . .] *all* social relations have a moral dimension to them, be they between parent and child, men and women, workmates, friends, neighbours, strangers, traders, people of different cultures, and more. (2005: 167; emphasis in original)

Sayer's point is that shame is a manifestation of social sentiment and particularly revealing in terms of the workings of social class. By the same token I would argue that anxiety is a highly social sentiment and that it reveals more about gender relations and relationships across generations than about social class. The expression of anxiety, which is often a characteristically feminine mode, reveals competing pressures and responsibilities, but often in a context where the anxious person is not sufficiently powerful to find a solution to the conflict. So anxiety and powerlessness are intimately linked. There is of course a difference between an occasional sense of anxiety (e.g. going for a job interview) and the chronic anxiety that can be a feature of on-going connections. I explore the latter through the following story, narrated by Maja as part of a study of parent-child relationships.[5]

Maja was born in the former Yugoslavia shortly before the start of the Second World War. As she said of her early years:

> We really lived very comfortably and – well, we had a nice life. Then 1941, when the war started, my father – because of being an officer – he had to join the war so he went into the war and my mum was left with three children. And he used to come home from time to time,

which I don't remember, I was very young, and then 1944 he left completely because Yugoslavia was taken by the Communists and he had to leave the country, and my mum was left with us. Our house was bombed – we were left on the street with no friends, no family, nobody around because my father [had] left, so my mum was left with three of us on the street actually without anything. And that was August 1944 and we were two weeks on the streets without roof over our head, without food, without anything. So my mother – because my father was like commanding some people, they knew him because he was the main man, so the ladies said to my mother if you want you can come to our village which is outside of the city and you can stay there during the winter and then in springtime you can go back and see what we can do. So we went to that village and they gave us one room. They didn't have anything as well because the war was still going on and they just put hay down on the floor and we slept there all four of us – three children and my mum. All winter we spent there.

Maja's father was eventually interned in England and about a decade after the end of the war her mother was allowed to join him. Maja and her family had suffered much hardship by then and her father died within a year of her coming to England. However, she met a Yugoslavian man who was somewhat older than her and she married. He was her first and only 'boyfriend'. They had one child, a daughter and they geared their lives towards providing security and the best possible advantages they could provide for the child. To continue with Maja's words:

I mean that was the first time that I had something of my own. My house, and, you know, my family, we tried really hard at that time not only us I mean everybody was [working] hard. You didn't have anything; you had to start from scratch. We both had to work and the wages were very little, but anyway we lived the life the majority of people did live. We worked and we tried our best. We wanted to bring her up and we very much wanted her to go to university and have a good life, good job.

Maja had faced a great deal of insecurity in her life and she had also had to work at various times to boost the family's income. Along with many Middle European migrants to Britain after the war, she was able to invest in her child in the knowledge that there were opportunities for her primary education and further qualifications, and ultimately for work at a higher level than she or her husband could have achieved. But there was a threat to her plans associated with her daughter's teenage years: because her daughter Ana was born in England and went to school there, she took on board many of the values and aspirations of her peer group at a time when young people were experiencing far more freedoms than any child (whether in Yugoslavia or the UK) had before the war. Moreover, by this time Maja's parents had died and she had no close family nearby. Her response was to try to be very strict with Ana and to impose on her limitations and restrictions that were quite out of line with those imposed on her school friends. Maja would not let Ana bring her friends home, would not let her wear fashionable clothes. She was attempting to impose upon her daughter the kinds of values she had grown up with in a very different context at a very different time. However, in due course Ana ceased to follow her mother's instructions. As Maja recalled:

My husband used to work night shifts then – this is now when Ana is already sixteen, seventeen, and nearly going to university and he was working nights, and she used to ask me if she could go out with her friends. I says 'Ana, O.K., I'll let you go, but please come home [by] ten o'clock.' She says 'Mum, they start at ten o'clock.' I says 'Please, Ana, just for the sake of arguments and all this.' And you know she used to go – and hours going through hell. I thought I wouldn't – I told my husband next day that I let her go but she was home on time. I didn't tell him, sometimes I let her go out without telling him and I was terrified because I thought if he finds out he'll say 'You ruined her life, you did this' – and I used to wait for her, I used to stand next to the window, turn the lights off so she can't see me, and that was [when] I saw these boys came, two boys with her and a friend, and I thought 'Oh my god, where has she been, what has she been doing.' It was terrible really. I was terrified all the time. We did let her out a bit. Maybe not as much as she wanted, and then really and truly I thought it would be best for all of us if she went to university away from home. She'll get her independence and I'll get – it's easier because she's not there,

I'm not waiting for her to come home, which I couldn't. I started with terrible migraine headaches. I had horrible migraine headaches. I was sick twenty times a day and the more I worried about something the more I had these attacks.

Maja's encapsulation of the anxiety she felt during this period of her life is vivid. She was trapped between a number of competing fears and obligations. She knew that her husband would hold her responsible if Ana got pregnant. She was in fear of his anger and blame about that possibility as well as the arguments that would ensue if he knew Ana had come home late. So she deceived her husband to avoid conflict, but doing so merely increased her worry. She became completely isolated with her terror. Her fears also rested on her conviction, which had been drummed into her as a young woman, that men wanted only one thing and that once they had had it, they would desert a girl:

> My Gramp used to always say 'No boys, the boys are always – they'll just get you in [trouble], or be nice to you till they get what they want, and they leave you and if you go from boy to boy you'll never get married, you'll never have a family,' and if you have baby before you're married – that's something my dad always used to say to me – 'If you get pregnant before you're married I'll kill you and I'll kill myself.' I would never, ever dreamt to have sex before marriage. That was something forbidden, and that was so deep in me that I believed that same thing for Ana. And as I was seeing it – I mean it wasn't as bad as it is now – but then if someone did get pregnant at Ana's age, and I thought if that happens to Ana I don't know what I'd do. It was so terrifying to me, so – I can't explain it to anybody – and that was the main thing, that really I was terrified that if she went out – I thought 'Oh my god I hope she's not with a boy.' I used to tell her that as well. I says 'Ana, boys are only after one thing, and if they get that they leave you.' She says 'you always put me off boys.' As I say again, I don't know, even now, if that was the right or wrong way to do it. But I believed in it, I was drilled in it, and I was drilling it into Ana, and I says 'No sex before marriage, that's terrible.' And I says 'You don't have anything to look forward if you have . . .' you know I was really drilling it into her.

It is clear from this passage that Maja was caught between different value systems, different cultures and different cultural moments. When she was fifteen she was still being raised by her mother and grandparents in Yugoslavia and her grandfather was the patriarch who imposed very stern standards regarding sexuality. But Maja was raising her own daughter in England in the late 1970s and few of Ana's school friends would have had parents who felt quite such intense fear in relation to their daughters' chastity. Maja was powerless in this situation and her response was, not surprisingly, to have migraines and to suffer bouts of sickness because of her anxiety. Maja says that she could not explain her anxiety to anyone because she was so isolated, yet she is able to convey it vividly in the interview. Even though all this took place at least twenty years beforehand, her recollections of the anxiety she felt were still very much alive. Maja had no financial independence from her husband, and in any case she was dependent upon him as the person who could look after them in what was still a 'foreign country' as far as she was concerned. Moreover, Maja's reference points remained in Yugoslavia. Given that she had engaged in paid work only intermittently in England and that she had spent only one miserable year at school at a time when she could not speak English, she had no way of incorporating different values in her life. She loved her daughter but could not communicate fully with her because her experiences (and education) were so different from her own. So the intensity of Maja's anxiety was also related to the fact that she was a first-generation migrant who had few kinship networks or friends to call upon for help.

Maja's story conveys strongly the gendered responsibility for sexuality and sexual honour that existed for women in her position. Her fears for her daughter speak volumes about the existing double standards of sexuality and the extent to which young women can be valued almost solely for their chastity.

Similar feelings of anxiety were expressed in interviews with two generations of Pakistani, Indian and Irish migrants that we carried out in Bradford and Leeds in 2002–3.[6] In particular parents were worried about their children taking on different values and failing to honour their own cultures and/or religions. While such emotions and concerns are not unfamiliar, the point about Maja's account is that it reveals the internal family dynamics and the personal costs associated with trying to manage such anxieties. Maja lived with these fears for years and her solution was to let her daughter go to university in another town, where she would not have to witness Ana's worrying behaviour and need not feel the immediate anxieties of a mother's responsibility. In other words, the solution was a form of separation, notwithstanding her love of and desire to protect her daughter. After some years of living apart (Ana travelled and Maja and her husband moved to the USA for several years), Maja moved back to the same town as Ana so that she could be close to help with her grandchildren. The mother-daughter relationship was restored but both Ana and Maja report that they carry with them the memories (and resentments) which that conflictual period induced. They were able to get away from one another, and this emotional ebb and flow saved their relationship, enabling it to be resurrected in due course. Mother and daughter were able to create a physical distance in order to preserve an emotional closeness. However, as I now go on to argue, the opposite position, namely emotional distance combined with physical proximity, can be equally problematic.

Living with hurt and distress

Interviewer: What would they [parents] argue about?
Ben [aged sixteen]: Everything.
Interviewer: But it doesn't worry you?
Ben: *I can't be bothered* to let it.
Interviewer: But did it before?
Ben: Yes.
Interviewer: But now you see it in a different light?
Ben: Yes, I see it as pointless; they can do it if they want to.

Interviewer: What about birthdays and Christmas, does dad remember that at all?
Jenny [aged fifteen]: He remembered the first one, and that were it.
Interviewer: How do you feel about that?
Jenny: *I'm not bothered.*

These two children were part of the project entitled 'Enduring Families', which was a follow-up study of children of divorced or separated parents whom we had interviewed some four years earlier.[7] Ben's parents were 'sharing' him on a virtual 50:50 basis, while Jenny had not seen her father for years (her parents had divorced when she was around nine). Ben found himself caught in a situation where, because his parents were still in regular contact with each other through a shared care arrangement, he witnessed their on-going conflicts: these would flare up whenever they had to negotiate anything. Jenny was in a very different situation because her father had never been much involved in her care and, as far as she was concerned, had shown very little interest in her. But both children, in totally different circumstances, were managing their situations by distancing themselves from the problem. Both were refusing to engage (or were attempting to avoid engaging) with the deteriorated relationships manifested by their parents' behaviour. Ben had come to realize that there was nothing he could do to change the situation and so reinterpreted the conflicts as his parents' problem rather than his. However, he still had to witness the arguments and had to go through an emotional and cognitive process to keep them from affecting him unduly. Ben was disengaged from his parents' relationship; he was in effect refusing to be part of a triad and related to each parent separately. Facing this kind of situation, many of the children we interviewed expressed a desire to leave home (in particular to go to university). This was less because they were having direct conflicts with their parents than because the emotional environment in which they lived was oppressive and negative. The following examples come from the project entitled 'Supporting Children at Times of Family Transition', in which primary school children were interviewed about their experiences.[8] In each case the children were responding to questions about what they did when their parents started to fight:

> **Benny** [aged ten]: [My brothers] don't care about it. Tara [sister] cares about it and she gets upset, but the boys don't. If they are watching the TV at night and [my parents] start arguing they just sit there . . . and ignore it.

Interviewer: So Tara will try to understand what is happening but Colin and James will try to ignore it, will they?

Benny: Yeah, because there are better things to watch on TV.

JJ [aged ten]: When they [parents] started fighting, I just turned my back. Just went to my room.

Miriam [aged ten]: I used to stuff myself with chocolate . . . to forget about it [parents' arguments] and watch TV 'til about three o'clock in the morning.

These children were all finding ways of ignoring or reducing the impact of very negative parental relationships being carried on around them. Their emotional (and practical) responses speak volumes about their powerlessness in their families: they could not leave physically, so they would leave emotionally, perhaps finding ways of consoling themselves – sometimes through eating and often through going to sleep. Miriam could leave her parents' home to go to her maternal grandparents who lived across the road, but once there she found her grandmother too would complain to her about her father, and blame him for events, and so she really did not have any escape. For some of these children the experience of their parents' arguing was a temporary phase, but this was not so for all of them. Moreover, although some found temporary relief because their parents separated, the rows could start again when a new partner was found. For others like Ben, whose parents were sharing his care, there appeared to be no escape at all.

Jenny's strategy of 'not bothering' was her way of distancing herself from a father she felt had rejected her. Her recollection was that he had rarely visited her after he had left her mother and, what was worse, he had ceased to remember special occasions like her birthday. She compared herself with her sister, whom she described as still caring about their father; but Jenny just found this emotionally punishing. Like the children who were trapped in conflict-ridden homes, children who felt that a parent (usually their father) had deserted them felt powerless to change the situation, nor could they get others to act on their behalf. All they could do was try to feel less concerned, since they could not act to change the situation. As Elise put it:

> **Elise** [aged ten]: There's nothing children can do [if parents split up]. It's because it's their parents. There's no point getting involved because it might make it worse.
> **Interviewer**: So what's the best thing to do?
> **Elise**: Try and forget what's happened and get on with normal life.

The power of adults to withdraw love and attention from children, especially in intact families, is hardly visible outside the family. Very few of the children in this survey were willing to talk to teachers or even school friends because to have been abandoned was an experience tinged with disloyalty and shame. This created a situation where many of the children faced the problem alone or, where other family members got involved, it often took the form of a Greek chorus commenting on the wrongs of the absent or wayward parent as the tragic narrative unfolded. This strategy by the wider kin could even make things worse. In the case of Josh's family, his father had left his mother for another woman and some ten years later his paternal grandparents were still discussing with him the inexplicable and unforgivable nature of his father's offence. Josh and his brother felt that they could not go to see their father, let alone stay with him, because it was their on-going duty to hate the second wife:

> **Josh** [aged seventeen]: We always talk about it, me and them two [paternal grandparents], we talk about how much we all hate her [father's second wife]. And they know him well, obviously, he's their son, and they still say, they would never say it to his face because they know it would break his heart, but they still don't know what he is doing with her because, they just can't see it in her, they just can't see what [he sees in her].

In the study about supporting children we gave a vignette to the primary school children in which a child is waiting for a father, who is late, to turn up for a contact visit. We did not imply that he was not going to arrive, we merely referred to the child as waiting and we asked what the child in the story might be feeling and what he or she might do. The children who were confident in their relationships with their fathers responded that he must have been held up and suggested getting their mother to phone him. For them it was a non-event, they hardly thought about it. But the children who had no confidence in their fathers responded very differently. They assumed immediately that he would not be coming at all and they empathized with the distress of the child in the story.

> **Kara** [aged nine]: [The father who did not turn up] might have got drunk and gone out with his mates and not caring about the son . . . I know how the little boy feels because my dad didn't want me at all, so I know how it feels.
>
> **Lizzie** [aged ten]: [The child in the story] just goes and lays on his bed and sleeps until morning. 'Cos I feel better when I wake up, forget about it.
>
> **Joely** [aged nine]: I don't care about [dad] any more because [of] everything he's promised; he lets me down all the time.

These responses suggest profound rejection and yet this is 'normal' life for some children. They appear to be trying to change themselves or at least their perceptions of the situation in order to cope. Alternatively, they reject the parent whom they believe to have rejected them. Some even spoke of the importance of forgetting and looking to the future, as if they could obliterate the bad things that had happened. In this vein, the strategy of going to sleep or watching television also appears as a clear tactic for keeping the feelings of hurt at a distance. Obviously this does not mean that these children are thinking about their hurt and distress all the time, but the sense of rejection could be called into being at key moments (e.g. when a birthday card fails to arrive) while also forming a dull backcloth to everyday life.

Living with disrespect and loss of self

The proverb 'familiarity breeds contempt' has been in English usage for a long time, conveying the idea that it can be difficult to sustain respect for someone once one has seen him or her in all sorts of conditions and states of mind (perhaps from infancy, during illness or inebriation or at any time of great stress). The children quoted above were beginning to show signs of disrespect for their warring parents (e.g. the television was more interesting) and, in these contexts, it is quite probable that the parents were displaying a lack of respect towards each other as well as to their children. But in contradistinction to the idea that familiarity is a problem is the idea that the family is supposed to provide a context where one can be most 'oneself'. This can involve all sorts of behaviour: saying things one might not say 'outside'; sharing views, secrets and opinions; not bothering to smarten up or shave; eating from trays in front of the TV and so on. These may be harmless forms of relaxation, but it may also mean that family members see each other at their worst as close kin may sometimes be prone to dispense with politeness and civility too. So there is a contradiction within families because they are places where people get close to one another; but closeness in a context of absolute privacy and considerable power inequalities can entail a certain amount of risk. Getting to know someone intimately over a number of years does not automatically mean that one likes what one finds. In particular it may be hard for parents to be both intimate and physical with their children, and yet to respect them as separate individuals with their own views and emergent values. It can also be hard for children who come to discover that their parents have feet of clay, to continue to respect them, especially when they see their parents doing the sorts of things they are forbidden to do. Yet without some degree of respect, the quality of relationships can become very problematic.

Giddens (1992: 192) has addressed the issue of democracy in families, depicting a shift away from vertical authority as held by the head of household who can command respect towards a style in which family members have more equality, where respect flows in all directions, not just upwards towards the male head. His might be an idealized image since empirically there is little evidence of equal and democratic family structures in Western cultures (Jamieson, 1948) but implicit in Giddens's argument is the idea that weaker family members should not be abused, ignored, disregarded or neglected. In other words, families need to achieve a balancing act between considerable familiarity and relaxed informal behaviour while maintaining the ability to respect the personhood of other family members.

Clearly I am not mapping out new ideas here. R. D. Laing (1969), for example, showed how psychologically damaging family life could be, most especially when parents refused to allow a child to become his or her own person and, in particular, when parents said one thing while actually meaning another. Laing's work on family relationships showed how powerfully families could both deny and distort the 'self', creating profound ontological insecurity: the child could establish no firm or reliable points of reference against which to understand the world or relationships. Laing's work focused on schizophrenia, but his case studies of family relationships held a wider significance because they showed the mechanisms (usually unintentional) through which the parent could fail to recognize the personhood of their child, and could send out contradictory messages which would mean that the child would always feel in the wrong. Such 'contradictory messages' are common where there is hostility and competition between parents. For example, in our interviews with the children of divorced parents, we found that it was not unusual for children to know that while one parent could express contentment that the child should visit (even love) the other parent, the parent with whom the child was domiciled was often miserable about the situation. In such cases it was small wonder that the children felt guilty about expressing affection for one parent or the other. Some children learnt how to deal with the kind of psychological pressures this could put them under.

> **Claudia** [aged twelve]: [T]hey always say I can say something but then, like, it's a bit hard you see because both of them want different things and if you agree with one, then the other one will feel a bit upset. I mean *they won't say that to you, but you can sense it* so it's a bit annoying. So even if you didn't want to do that, if you wanted to do something completely different, it's better to say [that] you want to do something completely different 'cos then neither of them wins, then they'll just find an argument about something else.

However, not all children, nor all adults, have the ontological security that Claudia reveals here. Being able to understand that what is said is not necessarily what is meant, especially when one is both dependent upon and in an intimate relationship with the speaker, can be incredibly hard.

These kinds of exchanges are extremely difficult to grasp in the ordinary run of sociological research on families. It is not just that what people say may not be what they mean: for people (parents and children) engaged in intimate relationships, it may be actions, looks or expressions rather than words that convey the significant meaning. As Andrew Sayer argues: 'Recognition is implicit in the way people address and deal with one another, whether they are kin, friends, associates or strangers, and in the merest looks of "civil inattention", as Goffman termed it' (2005: 55). Sayer continues:

> Moreover [. . .] recognition through deeds can speak louder than verbal recognition. I may *say* things that indicate recognition of you but if everything I *do* indicates insensitivity to your needs and disrespect of your intelligence and worth my words will be worthless. (2005: 56; emphasis in original)

It might be added that if parents regularly indicate this kind of insensitivity, it becomes particularly hard for children to have a sense of their own worth. Moreover, such problematic relationships can occur between adults, causing one adult to begin to feel worthless and to doubt her or his own intelligence or capacity to understand. Take for example this statement from a mother we interviewed in the *Family Fragments?* project (Smart and Neale, 1999):

> Kate: Plus there was a very important element of this victim cycle of abuse when [he] mentally and emotionally abused me for a long time. By the time we'd reached this point, I had absolutely no self esteem; I had no way of knowing that there was help out there, or that I could stop the abuse. There was nothing to tell me that I could actually get this stopped, that I didn't have to go through it. . . . some machinery in my brain was saying, 'He's going to be your abuser for ever, and there's nothing you can do about it.' That was the way I was

thinking, and it only took to see [my son] distressed to shake me out of that, but it took a long time to be completely free of that thought process.

Although this mother was separated from her partner, the abuse that had started during their relationship continued for a long time because the father had regular contact with his son. They continued therefore to be embedded in a toxic intimacy from which it felt impossible to escape. As Lynn Jamieson (1999) implies, in such awful relationships it is difficult to know where there is space for democracy or even recognition of the personhood of the other. It is also quite hard to develop a sociological analysis of the sort that Sayer carried out in his study of shame, or as I sought to do when looking at anxiety. Feelings of shame can be linked with class position, and feelings of anxiety with a gendered hierarchy and/or insecurity relating to the marginal position of the new migrant. These emotions can be traced to reveal normative structures around power and responsibility. The question is whether intimate enactments of rage or the felt experience of disrespect also have a wider sociological significance. In the former case, where parents might display their rage with each other in front of their children, forcing children to find strategies of avoidance or coping, it seems clear that the feelings that children express are linked to their powerlessness and their inability to influence the course of events in their personal lives. They are reduced to spectators quite often, but they are emotionally involved ones who recognize that their futures are at risk of harm. This powerlessness is in turn linked with the low status of children in general and also the power of secrecy, since children are aware that they should not let others know about some of the conditions prevailing within their families. The issue of disrespect may be analysed in similar ways, except that this involves more than generational difference. If disrespect is essentially about the denial of another person's personhood, then this can manifest itself in many ways, whether subtle or not. Recourse to violence is a tangible example, but there are less visible forms of corrosion of personhood that family life can foster. It is important to develop a sociological understanding of corrosive personal relationships because these are, in effect, the micro-workings of unequal power relationships which are sustained by the social and moral ordering of contemporary family life. It is equally important to recognize that not everyone can walk away from these relationships and that they are as much a part of the relational landscape as supposedly more 'modern' and more democratic relationships.

* * *

In this chapter, which explores the dark side of everyday family relationships, I have focused particularly on anxiety, hurt and disrespect because these were the issues that emerged from various sets of interviews. I have brought them together here as a means of highlighting everyday difficulties. I have not explored every kind of problematic relationship, nor have I sought to argue that the examples described above are typical or necessarily common. Rather my point has been to throw light on some of the problems that family members, especially women and children, have to endure on a daily basis. I have quoted extensively from interviews with children in order to evoke what might be called their everyday unhappiness, not only major events or trauma. The very ordinariness of this unhappiness needs to have a place in the sociological imagination. In focusing on the everyday experiences of women and children I do not mean to give the impression that men do not live with unhappiness. Instead I have attempted to show ways in which sociologists can become more attuned to these issues, while not abandoning a broadly sociological approach. Hence I relate the experience of anxiety to wider issues of gender, power and also migration/isolation. Experiences of hurt and disrespect are here related to questions of generation, age and power, in particular the way in which children have to manage these problems because they cannot influence the adults around them.

Most of the children we interviewed who were in negative family relationships could not wait to leave and most of the unhappy adults longed for some kind of escape. But I have argued that these relationships are tenacious; the bonds are seldom easily broken, not only because of issues of power and lack of resources, but also (as argued in previous chapters) because family relationships form a poignant part of our selves. The memories being laid down in these childhoods do not seem to be the warm or ontologically comforting variety of those discussed in chapter 4, and are unlikely to be recalled with joy in adulthood. It is therefore important to include understandings of how grim families can be and to remember that intimacy can be toxic and even destructive of the self. An exploration of the existence of, and significance of, negative emotions is an essential corrective to the growth in nostalgia about families in the past and also the taken-for-granted assumption that families are healing and supportive places.[9]

7

Possessions, Things and Relationality

In this chapter I explore a different aspect of relatedness and embeddedness in relationships. In particular I examine 'things', namely those apparently inanimate objects which are part of everyday life but which, as I argue (following DeVault, 1994), play a part in the construction and reconstruction of intimacy and personal relationships. The 'things' I pay attention to fall into two categories. The first, which includes the home and personal shared possessions within the home, represents forms of investment in relationships, while the second, including food, money and consumable goods, is concerned with forms of exchange within relationships. These are differences of degree rather than substance, since clearly possessions can be exchanged or given away, but the ways in which the investment and the exchange type of object operate tends to be slightly different. However, before progressing to my main discussion, it is necessary to map out some of the general issues that have been raised in thinking about things sociologically.

Aafke Komter (2001) has argued that sociology needs to develop a more refined 'sociology of things'. She acknowledges the foundational work of social historians and social anthropologists (e.g. Miller, ed., 1998) as well as the work that has taken place within the sociology of consumption (e.g. Corrigan, 1997), but her interests also lie in how social action gives meaning to things and how 'meaning derives from the nature of social relations' (2001: 61). Things, particularly in the process of exchange (a gift) or movement (moving home), throw light on social relationships because of the meanings that social actors give to them. Thus, for example, one might demonstrate that one cares for another person by finding him or her a particular, thoughtfully chosen gift. But more than this, meanings derive in turn from social relations. The exchange of gifts may be more or less appropriate depending upon the nature of the social relationship between the parties. So, for example, a paediatrician may care a great deal about a young patient, but would feel it was professionally inappropriate to offer that patient a present. Things therefore can throw light on social relationships in a number of ways, and for Komter the most significant route for sociology would be the latter, namely to focus on the ways in which meanings derive from social relations.

In pursuing this route Komter relies upon the work of Alan Fiske (1991), who has argued that there are four fundamental models of motivation in social life, namely 'community sharing', 'authority ranking', 'equality matching' and 'market pricing'. I shall explain what these mean below, but it is important to note first that Komter's approach is to define a sociological perspective in terms of a grand theory, which is argued to be 'universal' and applicable in all circumstances. This seems somewhat out of step with the poststructuralist turn that is evident in most contemporary sociology, but Komter appears to be using these models as helpful analytical categories in the analysis of her own empirical data rather than as articles of faith. This means that she strives to understand the meanings that people give to things by reference to socially structured relationships, and not only in terms of personal meanings. The community-sharing model is the domain of friendship, kinship and solidarity. Here things may be given without an expectation of return, and possessions and gift exchange have a sentimental value. The authority-ranking model is characterized by inequality; for example, possessions may become symbols of power and prestige and thus may be seen as markers of either superiority or inferiority. In equality matching the relationships are considered to be between peers; people either take turns or ensure that an equal balance is maintained. Market pricing is the category in which the most important criteria are utility and cost (or market value). Using these models to throw light on any given culture shows that a 'thing' can carry very complex meanings, which in turn can illuminate social relations. For example: a husband might give his wife an expensive necklace on their wedding anniversary; the jewellery may represent the fact that he loves her dearly (community sharing), but it may also reflect his status as a highly paid employee and hers as a housewife without access to her own income (authority ranking). Unless she can reciprocate with, for example, diamond cufflinks, there is no indication of equality. Now this lack of equality might not have mattered at a personal level in, say, England in the 1950s, but it might now cause disapproval. Far from being inanimate or 'innocent', things are imbued with meanings derived from the social context and social structure in which they occur.

Interestingly, Komter argues that she is more interested in things as 'depositories of *social* and *cultural* meaning' (2001: 60) than of *personal* meaning. However, as Finch and Mason (2000) have shown, personal meanings (such as how one interprets the quality of a relationship) may be vital in understanding the meanings that are salient at a given time. I explore this further below, but it is important to stress here that personal meanings are not less sociologically important. Moreover, it becomes important to understand how personal meanings iterate with social and cultural meanings, since they do not operate in separate or parallel universes. As Finch and Mason (2000) argue, there is no automatic symmetry between social and cultural values and personal ones. There might, for example, be a cultural expectation that the wife in receipt of the necklace in my example above should express increased gratitude and love towards her husband in return. But if she knows that the gift is intended to disguise his affair with another woman (or assuage his guilt about it), or if his expectation is that he gets something in return, the gift might contribute to a severe deterioration in the relationship. It is thus possible for things to vibrate with both social *and* personal relational significance. With this in mind I now turn to the core areas delineated above, starting with the meaning of home.

The home

The sociology of family life has paid quite a lot of attention to 'the home' (Allan and Crow, eds, 1989; Morgan, 1996; Chapman, 1955; Mallett, 2004), and feminist work, in the 1980s in particular, concentrated a great deal of effort on redefining the home as a gendered arena of work and potential oppression. Starting with one of the first mainstream sociological examples, it is possible to see that Dennis Chapman's book *The Home and Social Status* was a paean to early empirical sociology in the UK. A detailed study of homes and furnishings (mainly) in Liverpool in the 1950s, it set out to measure social class and status according to finely calibrated measures based on such issues as whether a house was a 'semi' or a terrace, whether the external pointing was in good repair, whether the floors were covered with lino or Axminster carpets, whether the dimensions and numbers of rooms reached an acceptable level, and so on. The study reveals much about the social and cultural values placed on different types of homes and furnishings in the post-war decade, but of course the values are those expressed by Chapman and his team rather than by the families involved. It was the research team who put a numerical score on each type (and style) of possession. Although survey results were also reported in the study, the personal meaning of a fitted Axminster carpet as compared to a rag-rug was not at issue; the focus was on the social meaning, which in turn was treated as self-evidently decipherable by the social scientist. The meanings held by the inhabitants of the homes studied by Chapman were deduced only indirectly and played little part in the final picture. It would of course be unfair to criticize this study carried out in the 1950s from the vantage point of half a century later because the research agenda and the nature of the sociological enterprise has changed substantially in the intervening decades. What was important about the study was that it took the minutiae of everyday living to be sociologically significant. Where people shopped for their furnishings, how they paid for them, what use they made of their rooms and many more fine details were all treated as sociologically valuable, even if the readers did not learn a great deal about the people who lived in the houses. Moreover this book set the tradition of studying housing and housing conditions in relation to social class and poverty. Thereafter it became more usual for sociologists to study housing rather than homes and so some of the detail that enthused Chapman became less important. In addition housing became a key feature of post-war studies of social class (rather than status) and went on to feature in embourgeoisement theories as measures of social mobility and class aspiration (e.g. Goldthorpe et al., 1969). So the mainstream concern with the 'home' shifted towards studies of housing, housing conditions, life on new estates and in new towns, all of which reflected the kinds of large-scale social changes of policy that were taking place in the 1960s and 1970s in the UK and elsewhere in post-industrial societies.

The sociological interest in the interior life of homes was taken up by feminist sociologists, who became interested not only in the gendered division of labour within the home, but also in the exercise of power within what became known as the private sphere. This latter redefinition of the home as the private sphere was significant theoretically for attempting to give equal weight to the private and public spheres – thus bringing the private on to the (then predominantly Marxist) sociological agenda. It also pointed to the downside of privacy, where violence, for example, could occur without any protection being afforded to victims or shame being accorded to perpetrators. So feminist work strove to dismiss a commonsense or rosy view of the home by redefining the private sphere as both a place of work for women and a place of danger for vulnerable members. As a result, many studies were carried out on housework, domestic labour, child care, the double shift, domestic violence, sexual abuse, inequality (of food and money distribution), isolation, loneliness and so on (e.g. Finch and Groves, eds, 1983; Pahl, 1989; Oakley, 1974; Russell, 1984; Bernard, 1976). The term 'home' was rarely used because it seemed to carry with it unreconstructed, pre-feminist ideas of the home as an idyllic place or haven from the outside world (Barrett and McIntosh, 1982). Indeed a term such as 'home' came to be seen as part of an ideological package which included 'the nuclear family', women's oppression and compulsory heterosexuality. This meant that there was little positive to be said about homes and people's feelings about their homes – except in as much as they were necessary to provide shelter and the wherewithal to live a decent life. Possessions were seen in material terms and ownership of such possessions – particularly those of value – became seen as more important than feelings about them. This was entirely understandable because the belief that dependent wives shared their husbands' earnings and possessions was clearly revealed as fiction in the 1960s and 1970s, when the divorce rates were rising but women were finding that they were being left without a claim to the matrimonial home, or to any of the property therein. At this time

> married women could only claim a share in the matrimonial home if they had made a substantial *financial* contribution to its purchase. They could also only claim items of furniture and so on if they had actually paid for them. If their earnings had paid for food, heating bills and children's clothing while their husbands' earnings paid for the mortgage and household goods, they could not legally claim any beneficial interest in the property or its contents. Certainly any non-financial contribution such as housework and child care did not impinge in a direct way. (Smart, 1984: 78)

Feminist work was therefore concerned to reveal the gender inequalities which lay hidden within the private sphere, and the material value of homes and possessions were given priority over the subjective meanings given to them in sociological analysis at that time.

Allan and Crow's edited collection *Home and Family: Creating the Domestic Sphere* (1989) reflected rather different concerns. The essays were particularly engaged with such topics as the significance of the move towards post-war owner occupation, the impact of technologies of the home, and the extent to which the home was becoming increasingly privatized and separated from community. The book can be said to build on but move beyond the two important sociological moments outlined above, namely the era of Chapman with its documentary imperative and its treatment of 'home' as an indicator of status and the class system, and the feminist moment where the home was defined as the private sphere and as part of a patriarchal system of gendered exploitation. It also bridged two different but equally important sets of sociological issues. One was the impact of social change (i.e. living on an estate rather than in a slum) and the other the significance of home-making (i.e. expressions of love in household management).

Some of the contributors to *Home and Family* were attempting to add more nuanced layers to the picture of the home than had been created by previous work. Jennifer Mason, for example, argued: 'A full and rounded conception of the home should embody the experiential arena. [. . .] This involves understanding the home as material [. . .]; as spatial [. . .]; as temporal [. . .]; as "metaphysical", or pertaining to ideologies and values; as social' (1989: 103). The suggestion here is that sociology's approach to the home had not been particularly rounded, indeed it had focused almost exclusively on the material aspects; where ideological issues had been included, they were not the values and ideations of the inhabitants of the home so much as derived from grand theorizing about the nature of exploitation. Mason's study involved interviews with older couples whose children had left home and who were therefore engaged in the process of remaking their homes and finding new meanings for them. Although she was not using ethno-graphic methods, her approach leant towards social anthropology with its emphasis on how people created meaning in their homes. She also stressed the importance of the construction of meanings in relation to other people rather than simply in relation to social structures – notwithstanding the fact that the changes that her couples were going through were caused by events beyond their personal control (e.g. the cultural expectation that children will leave the family home). This meant that in the process of redefining their homes, these older couples were redefining their relationships and their own image of themselves as a couple. Although they remained parents, they were no longer actively engaged in parent-ing. Yet they wanted to avoid their homes becoming 'empty nests', which in turn would define them as 'former' parents. Mason's study therefore reflected a wide range of issues about the home from, for example, any given moment in the life course to gendered expec-tations to personal feelings. As Anat Hecht has argued:

> A house encompasses an array of different materials, from furniture and fixtures to ornaments and décor, collectively creating a dwelling

experience that is greater than the sum of its parts. For these are more than mere 'things' [. . .]. They are what transforms our house into our home, a private cosmos that houses our memories of bygone times as well as our hopes for what is yet to come. (2001: 123)

This idea of the home as something more than the sum of its parts is also perhaps what had been missing from previous sociological accounts – even though it may be evident in other approaches.

As Shelley Mallett (2004) has discussed, the term 'home' has been highly contested. It has been conflated with the concepts of family (especially the idealized nuclear family), household or shelter, and has been opposed to those of homelessness and mobility. It has also been seen as an ideological construct or simply as a physical place where people reside. As a result, much energy has been spent on teasing out a definitive meaning, or occasionally to find the specific meanings for different groups of people (e.g. women, men, children, migrants, ethnic minorities, the homeless) (see Chapman and Hockey, 1999; Rapport and Dawson, 1998; Somerville, 1992). Rather than rehearse again all these different meanings and arguments here, I choose to continue at the constructive end of the debate, where it seems that there is a recognition that home does not have a fixed meaning (Ahmed, 2000; Gurney, 1997; Dupuis and Thorns, 1998). Rather there appears to be a growing acceptance that home as a concept cannot be fixed, but has variable meanings which reflect such elements as the quality of the relationships which are associated with home, or a time of particular activity (such as home-making or childhood), or to do with movement (i.e. a sense of nostalgia for something lost even if it was not acknowledged during its currency). Home is therefore tied to memory, to relationships, and to events. Moreover, the significance of home can wax and wane: it is not a constant nor does it reflect some kind of biologically given yearning (although being homeless – as opposed to mobile or nomadic – may always be deeply troubling). Take these comments from people we interviewed for the project entitled 'Transnational Families':[1]

Mrigendra [Indian man]: Well my home is where I am – at the moment here. If by any chance I go to India I will consider it again my home. I can get on very easily wherever I go. I had some time in my past in my early life [when] I once became penniless and I went to a very poor condition in a remote place in India. In no time I had created my own society there and enjoyed [everything] around me because it is your attitude. If you are sweet, if you are kind to others, you get on with other people easily. So everywhere I go I find myself at home.

Corinne [Irish woman]: Home was where we were brought up. People used to laugh here and they'd say 'What are you doing for your holidays?', and I'd say 'Oh I'm going home.' I always said I went home and they'd say 'Your home is here', which it was, but it was a figure of speech, we always went home. [. . .] it was the home of my childhood.

Shabeen [Pakistani woman]: I know the people here I know the area, I like it here and I've got friends and family, I would probably move if [husband] got a job somewhere else and he wanted me to go with him but if I didn't need to then I wouldn't. I was born and brought up here this is home even if I moved to London tomorrow I would still call this my home, my dad's been here for over forty years and for him it's home as well.

These three passages reveal at least three different ways of thinking about home. The first defines home as a way of being and frame of mind, the second as the place of one's childhood, and the third as the place where one is established and feels comfortable. But what each definition has in common is that home is about relationships. Moreover, it is clear that one can have more than one home, even though in some sense this is mildly disapproved of. Thus Corinne's friends would correct her when she spoke of going 'home' for her holidays. Yet this discursive formulation is extremely common and people often say they are going home when going to visit their parents (even if they never lived in the place or house where their parents currently live). Moreover, our transnational family members spoke frequently of 'a home from home', which captures at a colloquial level the sense of being able to have more than one home. Living in more than one place did not, in itself, make these people feel transient, rootless or less embedded.

If we think about the concept of home as a part of the way in which people experience and make their relationships, we can begin to understand some of the conflicts that have developed over the meaning of home in academic discourse. For example, as noted above, feminists have pointed out that the home, far from being a haven for many women, can be a place of oppression and exploitation. Yet, as Peter Saunders (1990) has argued (in his research at least), women do not tend to speak of home in this way. He has been challenged by Craig Gurney (1997), who has shown that women may express ambivalence about the home; Gurney's research offers valuable insights into the complex layers of feelings that women may have, and in particular how they may change in relation to time and to life events. It is, after all, perfectly possible to hold very contradictory feelings about one's home, just as one may have contradictory feelings about relationships. Fiona Devine (1989), for example, indicated that one of the things that women enjoyed about being at home, notwithstanding the housework, was the ability to 'potter about' and manage their own time – at least if they worked part-time. And Sarah Pink (2004) sees the home as a place where women can exercise agency and creativity. On the other hand, women at home all day with small children could feel isolated and lonely – that is to say they did not have enough contact with others because so many other women were out at work. Equally those women who worked full-time could enjoy their homes less because the double shift put them under too much pressure. Thus relationships to the home were influenced by other demands and other relationships. Ultimately this means that it becomes important not to generalize about the meaning of home but to recognize the concomitant ebb and flow of emotions.

One of the most revealing studies of how the meanings of home are associated with relationships has been reported by Janet Finch and Lynn Hayes (1994). As part of a wider study of kinship and inheritance, Finch and Hayes explored what it meant when a home, whether that of parents or sometimes other kin, was left as a bequest in the deceased's will, especially where there seemed to be a presumption that the next generation would go to live there or stay living there. Although this was a small study from which it would be unwise to generalize, these authors found that in the main adult offspring did not want to move into their deceased parents' home. The home was associated with their parents' relationship with each other and even where there may have been nostalgic feelings about the home (for instance if it was associated with childhood) this did not mean that people wanted to step into, and live within, the aura of their parents' relationship. Although some family legatees expressed conflicting feelings, particularly guilt over selling a home that had meant so much to their parents, this guilt did not typically weigh as heavily as the dread of living with ghostly relationships.

In stressing that homes are both manifestations of relationships and form part of a relationship, it is important not to lose sight of the materiality of the home (Miller, ed., 2001). Miller argues that homes are a kind of compromise, between the people who live there, between the current occupiers and the previous ones, and between what can be afforded and what is desired. Thus he suggests that homes are not simple reflections of ourselves and, from my slightly different perspective, I would argue that they are not straightforward reflections of relationships. So homes still 'speak of' gender and generational relationships which are often in conflict and are always undergoing change. Although in our cultural imaginary 'home' is inevitably conjured up as stable at the emotional and relational level (because very few can afford to keep moving or keep redecorating), in fact home is no more static than personal relationships.

Possessions

As with homes, possessions too become invested with meanings as parts of relationships (Carsten, 2000; Hurdley, 2006). While it is possible to single out possessions in a way that acknowledges that some are purely personal and not shared (either literally or metaphorically), many possessions that are acquired, either at the point of home-building or as gifts or bequests, come to embody to a greater or lesser degree elements of relationships. This constructed character of possessions may not be visible or apparent in the normal course of events, since many possessions are taken for granted and may sometimes be barely acknowledged, except perhaps in their use value. But when a home is burgled or damaged by fire or flood, the meaning of many possessions can spring into sharp relief. It has been pointed out (Miller, ed., 2001) that the meaning of possessions (and recognizing which possessions are most meaningful) cannot be objectively recognized; to the outsider the meaning of things has to be explained because it is often either buried in memories or has come to symbolize something unknown. I explore these meanings as they emerge at certain critical moments, starting with the study entitled *Passing On: Kinship and Inheritance in England* (Finch and Mason, 2000). Next I go on to consider what happens to possessions (and the meanings attached to them) when couples divorce or separate. These are both critical moments which reveal what is otherwise ignored, taken for granted, or even rather subliminal.

Finch and Mason place a lot of significance on the meaning of the bequest of possessions in a will:

> The emphasis here is on the symbolic rather than the material importance of the inalienable possession (some may be materially valuable, others not). Seen in this light, inheritance is fundamentally about the human condition rather than about economic wealth or power. (2000: 15)

Their study can be seen as part of the movement in sociology away from seeing 'things' in purely economic or material terms. Of course, this is not to say that the symbolic has not always had a place in some sociological understandings, but Finch and Mason here pursue this theme in order to reinstate the significance of symbolic meaning into understandings of kinship relationships. They explore issues concerned with making wills, deciding who should receive what, and also interrogate people's feeling about inheriting 'things' with an important distinction made between 'keepsakes' and 'heirlooms'. Keepsakes are those things most invested with meaning and often memories of a deceased loved one. The keepsakes invoke that person or some event involving that person, thus conjuring up feelings and reminiscences which keep the memory of that person alive. As noted above, the keepsake need have no monetary value because its preciousness lies in its personal associations. By contrast, heirlooms are inherited items which have lost or never had much meaning in the relationship between the original owner and the receiver. Thus, a piece of jewellery which originally belonged to a maternal grandmother may have less significance to the receiver than something similar from a mother. Finch and Mason note that some people felt duty bound to keep heirlooms because they might have been meaningful to a parent, even if the meaning is lost on their own generation or the next. 'Things' can easily lose their meanings if they are not reinvested in through a living relationship. What is more, 'things' which acquire these kinds of meaning tend to be personal possessions rather than items of utility. So everyday items such as irons, vacuum cleaners or lawnmowers are rarely accorded any level of symbolic meaning. Oddly, however, these things may take on symbolic meanings at the point of divorce.

It is odd that there has not been closer sociological attention paid to the immense difficulty that people encounter when they are dividing their 'assets' and possessions having decided to divorce or separate. Divorce courts have been preoccupied with this problem since the inception of the legal procedure and especially since wives were allowed to keep some of the property and possessions accumulated during a marriage (Smart, 1984). The division of property and possessions has a very important economic component, but problems in dispersing and sharing 'things' can arise over items of little monetary value because they have acquired symbolic significance. Such items as photograph albums or joint gifts or the DVD collection can all cause considerable pain and anguish even if some of them are replaceable. As Jean-Sébastien Marcoux put it: 'Considering that things embody relations and memory and that memory is selective, it follows almost logically that the sorting out of things becomes a metaphor for the sorting out of relations and memories' (2001: 83). Although Marcoux is here referring to sorting out possessions in the context of moving house, the point is even better made in relation to divorce (when at least one person and maybe both have to move house). At divorce or separation one is forced to sort out relations and memories rather than choosing to do so and, in being obliged to share out possessions, one is constantly reminded of hurt and pain, possibly also guilt and regret. Objects that were originally acquired as a joint symbolic investment in the future (a pepper mill, picture frames, cushions) all take on much more than their monetary value. Larger and more clearly valuable possessions such as a car may also take on very symbolic meanings as the loss of the car to one partner could also mean the loss of independence, which could be highly significant at such an emotional time. This forced sharing out of possessions is in effect a dismantling of what was planned to be a joint future, so the 'things' might in many instances come to represent the past and also the lack of a future. Moreover, notwithstanding the emotional significance of 'things' imbued with memories, the memories themselves may undergo transformations from recollections of joyful times to upsetting reminders of a relationship that has collapsed. So objects come to symbolize bitterness even where once they invoked happier feelings. In such circumstances people may opt to throw previously cherished things away, or even to destroy them. Clearing away the 'clutter' of previous relationships often comes to symbolize a way of 'moving on' and starting again.

Janet Carsten has also pointed to the way in which 'things' are not only mnemonic but can be part of the process of identity construction. There is a sense, she argues, that we are what we remember, and what we remember is often held fast by objects such as photographs, items from childhood, wedding gifts and so on. In her interviews with adults who had been adopted in childhood she found that her interviewees kept keepsakes which were themselves symbolic of time and endurance which were also vital to their understandings of kinship and relatedness. She states:

> A striking feature of many of the interviews I conducted was the frequent recourse made to visual artefacts of various kinds, to the letters, photography, poems, official documents, articles of babies' clothing [. . .]. The visual artefacts which were regularly produced out of a special box, suitcase, or file for my inspection were a literal production of history. Like objects in a museum, and similarly marked off from everyday objects, they gave historical depth to current versions of the identities of those I interviewed. (2000: 691)

If things like the home and personal possessions can be seen to be invested with relational meanings and also identity construction, while also reflecting wider social relationships as Komter argues, then it is also possible to see how things which are the currency of exchange in relationships also convey and create meaning. Komter's own research was about gifts between family members and friends, but the concept of exchange is wider than this kind of transfer. So in the next section I focus on the sharing of food and money within relationships, drawing on the research of others, but also on some of my own previous research.

Food

Marjorie L. DeVault (1994) has argued that the work of feeding the family is part of the process of producing the family. By this she means that meals and meal times are moments of intersection when all (or a subset) of family members come together, while for the rest of the day they may be doing quite separate things outside the home. However, she also argues that people do not 'come together' naturally or automatically: what brings them to the intersection is the organizational work of the person who feeds the family, namely the mother. DeVault's study of the work of feeding the family is particularly concerned to establish that shopping (provisioning), cooking and feeding are all forms of work, and in turn these are primarily forms of women's work. In line with studies of housework (Oakley, 1974) and caring (Graham, 1983), she emphasizes the significance of gender and the invisibility of women's work. She believes that because eating is thought of as natural, and because meal times tend to be a cultural routine, the reproductive work that goes on behind the scenes is completely overlooked. Yet it is the reproductive work, which DeVault argues to be feeding work *par excellence*, that creates the family and organizes the relationships between family members. Seen in this light, the preparation of food and meals can be seen as pivotal in constructing the home as a special place. For example, DeVault cites those wives/mothers who prepare special meals to make 'coming home' feel welcoming and desirable.

Several authors (e.g. DeVault, 1994; Murcott, 1983; Charles and Kerr, 1988) have touched on whether food preparation is a form of pleasure or of drudgery for women. This is a complex issue and can be seen to depend a great deal not only on material resources, time resources, skill and creativity, but also on the amount of gratitude and pleasure that might be given and/or received as part of the process. But this emphasis, and the focus on women as servers of food, has to be understood as a particular preoccupation of studies of that time: Debbie Kemmer (2000) argues that most studies of food and families focus on domestic arrangements at a time when there are young children in the home and also when women are less engaged in the labour market. In addition she points out that such studies as those by Murcott and Charles and Kerr were carried out in the 1980s, and aspects of gender relations, especially in households without children, may have changed since then (Sullivan, 2000). So Kemmer argues against adopting a timeless view of women as the servers of food and as deferential to their husbands' tastes. In their article of 1998, Kemmer and her co-authors looked at a small number of heterosexual couples who were just beginning to co-habit and they found a greater sharing in the tasks of shopping and cooking, while also noting that women still took on the nurturing role. But most significantly for my argument here, the symbolic value of having a meal together was found to remain significant. So in this regard, the emphasis placed by DeVault, Kemmer and others on sharing meals and the role that this plays in creating a certain kind of relationship seems to have remained unchanged.

However, Alan Warde suggests that even the symbolic meanings of food preparation and eating are subject to change and need not be a timeless and relentless part of reproducing family relationships. He examines recipe books and advertising in relation to food preparation and notes how the messages contained in these media changed from the 1960s to the 1990s. As advertisers came to realize that women were experiencing greater time pressures than before, the emphasis on feeding (particular kinds of food) and the need for preparing home-made meals lessened. He argues:

> The reduction in reference to the familial and the home-made is remarkable [. . .]. It suggests by default, the importance of the various aspects of convenience to food preparation now, and a desire on the

part of the magazines to avoid being disparaging about saving time. The implication is always that women should, if they wish, be excused the obligation to perform the domestic role of carer. And the magazines are careful not to expose women who make this choice to unnecessary guilt. (1997: 138)

Warde also points to other shifts over time, for example for some social classes at least from feeding the family towards cooking and food preparation as part of entertaining and socializing outside the family. Meals themselves have shifted (again for some social classes) away from the home towards restaurants. This means that even if the symbolic significance of meals at home remains important, there are other eating practices which work in parallel and may develop their own symbolic significance (for example the meal out on an anniversary or birthday).

The meaning of the family meal has, in the first decade of the twenty-first century, become a site of ideological conflict which suggests also that neither the practice, nor the meaning of these practices, are stable. Politicians and commentators on the family often bemoan the demise of the family meal, attaching precisely the same significance to families eating together as does DeVault and the women she interviewed. In other words a shared meal is seen as a time of bonding and of bringing disparate members together for at least a short period of time. However, Murcott (1997) challenges the idea of the ubiquity of the family meal in the past and so she is also critical of the idea that family meals are giving way to solitary eating or grazing which in turn symbolize the decline in family life and relationships. She suggests that there is little evidence that families all ate together in the past; in particular the upper classes would seldom eat with their children. She also argues that in poorer families, shared meals could be a result of economy rather than a desire to be together; she points to biographical accounts that describe the misery of family meals at which parents would argue or where children were subjected to disciplinary cruelty. Murcott argues that the family meal has become an aspiration and a symbol that parents are parenting correctly, but she also points out that without more evidence, the idea that families once all did this together is part of 'Golden Age' thinking.

These debates suggest that the meanings accorded to food preparation and eating are subject to cultural pressures as well as being open to change at a more personal level. As Kemmer (2000) suggests, women are likely to invest less store in cooking for their partners if they see themselves as part of an equal relationship. Or perhaps the value of cooking for another when a relationship is equal resides in the degree of reciprocation. This takes us back to the topic with which this chapter opens, i.e. Komter's model of the reflection of social relationships in things. Studies such as Murcott's, carried out in the 1970s, may be said to have reflected the 'authority ranking' model where there was an unequal exchange between heterosexual partners, but those of the 1990s onwards (e.g. Kemmer et al., 1998; Kemmer, 2000) might suggest the 'equality matching' model.

Money

Money, even more than food, represents a highly symbolic exchange within families and personal relationships. The gendered nature of this exchange (at least within marriage) has been subject to both strict cultural norms and legal restraints in the UK until around the 1970s. Until halfway through the twentieth century, for example, married women were rarely in a position to own their own property and until 1964 non-earning wives were not entitled to keep *any* savings from their housekeeping money as it was deemed to be the property of their husbands (Smart, 1984). Practices of house conveyancing and tenancy assignment on social housing all gave legal rights (or ownership) to husbands and so women's access to and control over money has been traditionally circumscribed. This does not mean that women could not informally control household budgets, and in some cultures men would give their wage packet to their wives unopened – this was usually where there was considerable poverty and budgeting was an onerous task (Vogler, 1998). Jan Pahl's work on gender, households and money management, which started in the 1980s, has mapped the complex ways in which heterosexual couples have organized their finances in the context of changing mores around gender equality (1980, 1989, 1990; Pahl and Vogler, 1994). She has emphasized the complex ways in which different models of money management (e.g. having joint accounts, keeping separate accounts) and different patterns of expenditure might reflect not only gender difference but also power and inequality in heterosexual relationships. Her work has revealed money to be a subtle (and sometimes less than subtle) indicator of hidden power in relationships. But she has also pointed to the ways in which the meanings given to a style of money management, notably the idea that a joint account indicates commitment and true sharing, can actually obscure inequalities: for example, access to the account is often unequal; furthermore men and women may spend from it in very different ways.

A problem that arises from these studies, however, notwithstanding their important insights, is that the focus on 'objective' gender inequality tends to push the meanings that couples give to their own style of money management into the background. Thus, for example, the young mother who is at home with a small child might assert that there is absolute equality and sharing of money in the household; the researcher, on the other hand, may feel that she 'knows' that the husband who is in the labour market actually has control and can withdraw consent to the arrangement at will. Men's control over financial matters when women leave the labour market is well acknowledged and can be said to be one of the invisible structures of gender inequality. So this poses the question of what to make of the meanings that people themselves give to the exchange of money that occurs in intimate relationships. Should *personal* meanings be treated as less sociologically significant than *social* or *cultural* meanings? How should a financially dependent wife's rather awkward personal belief in equality be treated when manifestly her husband in the labour market has more economic power in the situation?

These questions are addressed by Charlott Nyman in a paper which attempts to go beyond established understandings of how money 'works' in gender relationships. Nyman introduces two new dimensions into the debate. The first is that money can acquire different meanings and that these meanings can change over time. Thus she argues that there is not an automatic or natural meaning associated with money but that couples can define different monies in different ways. Secondly she argues that non-pecuniary values can influence money:

> Money has traditionally been seen as capable of quantifying and corrupting non-pecuniary relationships, values, and motives. Yet, the opposite relationship, that non-pecuniary values affect the meaning of money, was, and still is, seldom considered. Zelizer (1989) argues that money can have a variety of meanings that regulate its usage. The earmarking of money is a vivid example of how different kinds of money are shaped by cultural and social factors. (2003: 83)

In arguing that personal meanings can challenge social meanings, Nyman indicates that we cannot automatically read off from labour-market patterns or different levels of gendered income that power will work in only one way. She acknowledges that power remains important, but sees it as negotiable, suggesting that women may trade power over money for power over other aspects of domestic life or relationships. The two extracts from interviews that follow give some indication of this negotiation.[2] Shaban, a British Pakistani woman, renegotiates the system of money management in the household by reference to her religion:

> **Shaban:** We keep our money separately now; we used to have it together for a long time. Then about five years ago, I decided that I wanted my money separately, I became more aware of my Islamic rights and his responsibilities and I felt that the way my money was used, was not giving me my full rights. What would happen was, we used to put all the money into a joint account and in theory we both made decisions on how it was supposed to be spent. But I felt I often had to argue very strongly for things that I wanted to spend money on and I felt he had too much control over my money. His response to that initially was 'Well you have to share the bills equally' and my comeback was 'No I don't, it's your job to provide for us in this house, if I help you with that, that is something you have to negotiate with me and it's something I do of my own free will not because I feel obliged to do it.' Since we've come to that agreement it has given me a stronger financial position through my Islamic rights rather than accepting a Western point of view that you both work

therefore you both share the bills. This would have put me into a very difficult position because I was obviously earning less than him, I couldn't work full time because of the children, so my Islamic rights gave me a lot more control over my money and what I did with it. For the past five years I have kept my earnings separately, I do help him with the household bills and generally I have the kids with me most of the time. When you have the kids with you, you end up spending left, right and centre. I spend a lot of my money on the children and spend money on things which we wouldn't have been able to give them before like private tuition, to support them in their academic work. I feel like I want to spend it that way even though that is expensive because I have control over my money. I am probably spending just as much but [. . .] I feel like I am doing what I want to do and what is good for the family as a whole.

Shaban negotiated a situation in which she insisted that her husband's income cover household bills and she was thus free to keep her own money to spend as she wished. Interestingly, however, it appeared she not only spent almost all her money on her children, but she also helped her husband out. But the point is that while her patterns of spending do not seem to vary greatly from the Western women she differentiates herself from, she acquired considerable self-respect as well as strength from being true to the teachings of her faith. Shamshaad, a British Indian woman, however, took a completely different stance:

Shamshaad: We need the money, at the moment my husband has had an operation and he is at home, so he's not working at all. But then he's never let me work.
Interviewer: Why do you think that is?
Shamshaad: He's always said 'That's why I'm here, you don't need to work.'
Interviewer: Did you want to work for other reasons, other than financial?
Shamshaad: No, like what?
Interviewer: For independence or something?
Shamshaad: No [laughter], what would I want with independence? My husband is a good man.

Shamshaad felt no need to work because she could trust her husband to provide for her and their children. Furthermore, she clearly felt that her husband treated her well and that she needed no potential 'escape route' or independent existence. For Shamshaad it seems that money had no more than financial meaning, while for Shaban it had religious significance with undertones of both independence and self-respect.

The idea that money, and the interpersonal power of money, can vary in different relationships is supported in part by Carolyn Vogler (1998). She argues that the way in which married couples organize their financial affairs is a reflection of certain ideologies (e.g. of equality) and that this in turn modifies the power that might otherwise accrue from the fact that husbands usually earn more than their wives and are in a position to control their earnings (Burgoyne, 1990; Burgoyne and Morison, 1997). So she challenges the idea that money is a crude index of power, even though she recognizes the disadvantages facing women with low incomes or whose earnings are treated as supplementary. Vogler does not reach as far as *personal* meanings however, and the ideologies she refers to tend to be broader social ideologies such as the traditional idea of the primary status of the breadwinner or the late twentieth-century ideology of gender equality. Yet she does raise the problem I note above, namely that of dismissing the meanings people themselves give to their actions and decisions in favour of an externally imposed understanding of 'real needs'. Some, for example, might argue that Shamshaad (quoted above) does not recognize her own best interests and that putting her faith in her husband to support her is (or might be) misplaced. But Vogler fights shy of this kind of assertion, noting an approach developed by Julia Brannen and Peter Moss (1991) in which it is taken to be the point at which women (and men) themselves start to express discontent in arrangements that suggests power relations are shifting. In other words, how couples themselves speak about the way in which money is organized should be treated as the most significant indicator of meaning. It follows that the extent to which they argue over arrangements might be a better indicator of conflicting interests than the researcher–imposed interpretation of gender inequality.

This raises the question of whether money, and its organization, has different meanings in same-sex couple relationships and households. Jeffrey Weeks, Brian Heaphy and Catherine Donovan (2001) have argued that same-sex couples aim for different goals when it comes to financial management. They suggest that the model most typical of same-sex couples is one of pooling money for joint or household expenditure, while keeping back the rest for personal spending. This they argue represents an ethic of co-independence in which there is sharing, but also each individual retains both control over some money and a sense of autonomy or separateness. We found this arrangement to be quite common in our study of gay and lesbian marriage as well.[3] Take Tina and Jo's response to our question about financial arrangements:

> **Tina:** We have a joint account that we pay for joint things out of but we both have a separate account as well. Which I think is really important because in a way it shows that we are two separate people but . . .
> **Jo:** It is about commitment.
> **Tina:** Yes, yes we both contributed to the running of both places equally and things like this, vet bills.

However, although we found that pooling some money for joint needs and keeping a separate account was common, what this actually expressed might have been rather more complex. Vogler (1998) points to the fact that it is not enough to pool money, one needs to know who controls it. And there are also significant adjustments to make in relation to how much is pooled and whether this is an equal amount or an equitable amount which reflects differences in earnings (Burgoyne et al., 2006). We found some gay men and lesbians who were perfectly happy to leave the control of money to their partners; they did not seem to put great store by the meaning of money as an indicator of equality or inequality. This might indicate that same-sex couples do not invest financial matters with that range of significance quite simply because they do not enter relationships with the historical, gendered, heterosexual baggage of cultural meanings around money (Heaphy et al., 1999). In response to our question about whether couples pooled their finances, we received some unanticipated responses:

Derek: No Aidan keeps it all. He has some stashed somewhere. When I am going away he says 'Well here is ten pounds for your spending money.'

Aidan: Yes we do, we do it by account.

Derek: Actually Aidan does all the bills, finances, and I just say to him shall we go out to the bank and he says yes.

Kurt: Yes [we share] everything. That [meant] a lot to me; [it] showed to me his commitment. Obviously he earns double what I do but from the beginning there was no issue about it. It was just like normal, we pooled our resources together which I was not used to. I have had a few relationships before him and it was never anything like that and when we met from day one it was *our* money which was actually his money but anyway.

Stella: Everything, we do not have anything that is separate, everything is in joint names and joint access. Absolutely everything I cannot think of anything [we don't pool] really. Even the pocket money really. Denise is the financial manager of the purse; I am not very good at it. 'Can I have two pounds to go for the paper?' 'You do not want two pounds, one pound will do.' Everything is pooled, absolutely everything.

What was interesting about the ways in which the couples we interviewed dealt with money was that for some, especially those in very long-term relationships, there was no special significance attached to who controlled the money. There were those who saw complete sharing as a sign of real commitment, while others saw this as a way of losing one's identity, but for most it did not seem to trigger such momentous feelings. Certainly if a working, heterosexual married woman said she had no real know-ledge of her financial circumstances and that she relied on her husband to give her money when she asked for it, it would indi-cate a distorted power relationship. But it is less clear that this is what, for example, Stella and Derek above are implying. Interestingly, in one instance a couple we spoke to decided to model their arrangements on those suggested to them by their straight friends:

Paul: Oh we pool expenses but we have separate accounts.

Dominic: Paul knows exactly to the cent what he has in his account and I have not got a clue what is in mine.

Paul: And that is going to stay the same, separate accounts yes. Quite a few straight couples have said to me that they have straight accounts[4] and they think that it is the best way of doing it.

Interviewer: Straight accounts?

Paul: What did I say? Oh yes, separate accounts. And they think that that is the best way of doing it.

Dominic: Yes but then others have just said that they are amazed that we do not have one [a joint account]. So it depends what you want.

Dominic's final comment, 'So it depends what you want', is particularly significant. It suggests that, notwithstanding some cultural pressures to conform to certain styles of money management in relationships, there is a greater (but not total) freedom for same-sex couples to do what they think suits them as a couple. Few individuals who referred to their partner as the money manager showed any embarrassment about the situation. By contrast with the findings in studies on heterosexual couples (married or co-habiting), it seems that the issue of equality (or inequality) for same-sex couples is established in relation to other matters and not in relation to money. This means that money does not appear to be hugely invested with notions of power and that it can be a more simple currency in the relationship.

★　★　★

In this chapter I have foregrounded the importance of inanimate objects or things and explored the part that things play in relationships. I have suggested that things positively resonate with meaning and also that we can understand the nature and qualities of relationships by exploring how individuals deal with things, especially possessions. This means that in addition to a traditionally sociological approach to material things (for example measuring wealth as an indicator of social power, or categorizing types of housing as a means of assigning social class) I have suggested that the more anthropological approach of looking for relational meaning in 'things' adds an important dimension to our understanding of personal life. Thus I have suggested that we can enrich our understanding of the significance of things like the home, meals or money if we explore the meanings that these 'things' have for people in their daily relationships. Thus I have argued that it is important to find ways to incorporate personal meanings as well as social and cultural meanings into the sociological approach. If sociology is to capture more clearly what matters to people in their everyday lives, it seems necessary to heed how they interpret their own actions and intentions.

This raises problems for sociological analysis because, as empirical researchers know, most people tend to have more to say about personal meanings and understandings than about social structure, the class system or even inequalities of gender and ethnicity. So, gaining access to personal meanings and giving these 'sociological status' is problematic if a broader view is not also incorporated. As Julia Brannen and Ann Nilsen argue in a different context:

> Silence about the structural side of the dynamic [between agency and structure] does not mean it is unimportant in people's lives. Rather structure and context form part of the taken for granted aspects of life that are omitted from people's narratives and accounts provided in the research encounter. (2005: 418)

This suggests that people may not ordinarily refer to structural issues because they are in some ways invisible or so obvious that they form a taken-for-granted backcloth. But, according to Brannen and Nilsen, this silence does not mean they are understood to be insignificant. In other words they suggest that just because people do not talk about, for example, class constraint or generational power, it does not mean that these are not present and important in their lives. The problem, sociologically speaking, is to get the balance right so that there is sufficient attentiveness to personal meanings, while not losing sight of things which are not said, namely the social and cultural dimensions. The converse is equally important, namely there is a need to have a vision which will incorporate the social and cultural levels, while not ignoring or distorting personal meanings and individual agency. The balance between these levels has tilted and shifted over the decades as different theoretical orientations have taken the ascendancy in sociological theory (compare the emphases of symbolic interactionism with scientific Marxism, for example). But personal meanings are now being taken seriously again and this is suggestive of a re-emergence of anthropologically inclined sociology as well as the influence of life-story methods, biography and ethnographic styles of research.

My focus on 'things' in this chapter is a part of this development and I have steered my arguments towards adopting a nuanced appreciation of the meaning of inanimate objects in the realm of personal relationships. I have taken time to consider how important ordinary and unremarkable things are in everyday life. Sociology's predominant emphasis on the material underpinnings of social life has ironically meant that the material has been valued almost exclusively in economic terms. A good example of this, as noted above, is the early feminist work on styles of money management in heterosexual relationships. Yet later studies have noted that people's own understandings may bring in different dimensions and meanings which deserve analytical incorporation, that the significance of arrangements may change over the life course rather than being static, and that as wider social change occurs the available meanings that people give to the same arrangements may be radically different. Following through the changing (shared and individual) meanings given to meals, cooking, home decoration, material objects, money, gifts and other possessions is a way of understanding how close personal relationships may change (or stay the same). It becomes possible to track issues of power and inequality, of pleasure, care and desire, and to consider whether or not 'things' can signify degrees of embeddedness and relatedness. This means that in the field of personal life it is important to incorporate analyses of 'things' and to recognize that everyday life is lived through things as part of the fabric of face-to-face relationships.

Conclusion

I see this book as the beginning of a process of connecting ideas and concepts in order to create an imaginative, multi-dimensional field of study known as personal life. In this conclusion I revisit some of the themes explored above, drawing them together to make a case for a new departure in how we think about and do research on relationships and families. I also reflect on the nature of this book and the way in which it has been written, since it is my view that both content and style can be important in developing new ways of thinking. It is of course necessary to acknowledge that in claiming 'newness' one always invites the counter-claim that nothing is ever new (or sufficiently new) in sociology, and that someone else has inevitably had these exact or similar thoughts before and might well have expressed them better or more profoundly. In any case, I hope that the way I have put these ideas together will contribute to fresh ways of developing and deepening the field.

One of my core aims in this book has been to foreground the areas of personal life that have been left in the shadows or on the margins of the discipline of sociology. To this end I have focused particularly on memory, biography and certain aspects of emotional life. I have made the case that relationships are really not comprehensible without embracing these dimensions; it is bizarre that so

many books have been written about families, relationships and
kinship without much mention of love (or hate) or other emotions
and feelings. Memory, too, has been an odd omission from sociological work, although this oversight is in the process of being cor-
rected through study of the ways in which personal memory can
create a sense of self, identity and social connectedness. My book
therefore brings together marginalized issues and quite deliberately
does not dwell on some of the more familiar terrain such as trends
in family structures, domestic labour or gendered divisions of care
work.

Another important aim has been more epistemological than substantive, namely to link empirical research with theorizing in a new
way. By this I mean that I have taken a view across several empirical research projects with which I have been closely involved, and
have identified themes that are pertinent to contemporary questions
about personal relationships. I have revisited many of the interviews
that I (or research team members) have carried out in order to interrogate the accounts we collected in different ways. This has been
possible only because my knowledge of the full range of data has
enabled me to recognize issues across projects and not just within
them. This in turn means that I am in a position to occupy a particular intellectual space by returning to narratives that I know well
rather than relying on reported outcomes from projects created by
other researchers. I have also avoided a narrowing of focus, which
can be a result of reporting solely on one project and its findings.
This has allowed for a kind of freedom to make links and to delve
deep into the knowledge that I can bring to bear on my critique of
more free-floating theorizations such as those I have classified as
individualization theories. I do not doubt that some will find this
approach problematic because nowhere in the book is there a
detailed account of each project, its methodology, its research questions and its findings. But that information is easily available from
the references I have supplied, and providing full details of all the
individual projects would have deflected from the aims of this book.

In these chapters I have also relied on different methods of
conveying or creating meaning. In places these are entirely conventional and consist of outlining and criticizing or developing
existing ideas and arguments. But I have also followed less familiar

routes in seeking to deploy the data evocatively rather than simply as evidence. Some of the ideas that arise in this way are suggestive rather than conclusive and this is because the studies were not designed to pursue the new research questions I may now have. But in rereading transcripts of interviews it is always possible to find new insights and, with the benefit of different conceptual frameworks, it is equally possible to use those ideas to open up new avenues.

I have also quoted verbatim quite extensively from these interviews. Ann Corden and Roy Sainsbury have explored the ways in which qualitative sociology has increasingly followed this practice and their study uncovers a range of complex meanings held by researchers when including such extracts. One important reason for doing so is the desire to 'deepen understanding' or perhaps to make more real the views of interviewees. As they put it:

> There was some belief that people's own spoken words sometimes made more impact than the researcher's narrative in conveying life experiences to readers. [. . .] For some researchers this belief was reinforced by response to their articles from readers, and their experiences at conferences when they had observed the impact of verbatim quotations presented as overheads during presentations. (2006: 13)

Corden and Sainsbury are fully aware of the difficulties and ethical balances that are essential when presenting verbatim accounts, but the growth in this practice does seem to signify that the 'presence of real people' in sociological narratives is seen as important. This reflects my own purpose in drawing extensively on interviews: I want to allow personal meanings to enter the text (no matter how imperfectly) as a means of reflecting everyday life. I have also relied on quotations to emphasize the importance of personal meanings – not just social or cultural meanings – to the sociological project. But such quoted passages can introduce ambiguity and ambivalence; they can disrupt the text. The presence of everyday speech and thought can reveal how sociological narratives smooth out contradictions and untidiness. It seems that in interviews people are allowed to reflect their social and personal worlds as messy and confusing, while it is the sociologist's task to impose order on this sometimes bewildering array of possibilities in her or his analysis.

The quotations can therefore create a tension with the clarity of a given argument but rather than this being a bad thing, it can remind us of the difficulties of melding together complex everyday life with clear explanations of such a life.

I have also ventured into sociological approaches akin to life stories and autobiography. My previous projects have not entailed 'pure' life histories and so the material collected was typically geared towards specific research questions rather than completely open-ended. But I have seen it as important to introduce, where possible, more depth to certain accounts in order to allow the reader greater access to the speaker's mode of expression, feelings and recollections. My use of the autobiographical voice is to some extent experimental but is a crucial part of my aim to acknowledge the interplay between the real lives of those researched and those carrying out the research. I thus bring together in one place different ways of knowing and understanding (no matter how imperfectly), which sometimes creates a collage effect rather than a conventionally logical, linear argument. I am aware that as a result my chapters do not all have the same shape or form: some sections are more likely to 'work' for some readers than others.

The challenge to a sociology of personal life is also to be able to reflect complexity and ambiguity without being confusing and incomprehensible. I believe that this can be achieved by thinking of analysis and subsequent explanation in terms of layers of meaning or threads which, when finally woven together, can capture (whether evocatively or descriptively) the actuality of personal relationships. The threads themselves need not be uniform or complex as long as the final picture is. The chapters above are deliberately intended to make a cumulative argument rather than to stand in discrete relationships with each other.

In this book I have also aimed to provide ways of thinking about personal and family life, relationships and intimacy, ways that do not fall into the snares laid by dominant debates on families and social change (e.g. individualization/de-traditionalization theories or decline versus progress). Although I have had to engage with these debates in order to establish my starting point, I have paid more attention to mapping new ways of thinking or of combining ideas. After more than twenty years of research in this field, I admit to being weary of some of the debates that recur in slightly different forms over and over again. This is why chapter 2 discusses relationships outside the usual frameworks. The overlapping conceptual fields of memory, biography, embeddedness, relationality and the imaginary suggest to me an exciting, interdisciplinary and intellectually flexible way forward. These can of course be combined with the more traditional sociological concepts of class, ethnicity, gender and so on, but the primary aim should, in my view, remain one of being attentive to what matters to people in the construction of their everyday lives. This approach allows for a different integration of the concept of agency, which I hope sidesteps the familiar arguments over agency and structure and, in particular, the criticisms of individualization theories that tend to extract the person from their embeddedness in history, tradition, biography and relationships. Agency is acknowledged and explored but always within webs of connectedness. If we give proper consideration, for example, to the social significance of memory in the cultural, historical and personal construction of the self, it becomes difficult to assert (at least without much more evidence) that people are becoming more individualized and autonomous from one another.

I have argued that one of the main reasons for identifying a new field of personal life in sociology is to transcend some of the debates and intellectual baggage that inevitably cling to concepts relating to the family. But I have also acknowledged that it is futile to think of banishing the terminology of 'family' because, as David Morgan (1996) argued over a decade ago, the associated ideas will not go away because they resonate with a host of cultural and personal meanings. Families do matter, whether real or imagined, and parts of this book – especially the discussions of memory and cultural transmission – emphasize just how deep-seated familial relationships can be for each new generation. So the sociological idea of personal life is not meant to replace that of the family; it is used here as an inclusive term which does not always have family as its starting point, finishing point or as an inevitable point of reference. Morgan developed the useful idea of family practices to try to demote 'the family' in the sociological imagination. However, I think it is now time to go further and to develop a broader conceptualization, one that can keep the term 'family' in the lexicon, but which puts it alongside other forms of intimacy and relationships without always already prioritizing biological or married forms of relationship and/or intimacy. I have suggested that developing a field designated 'personal life' incorporates all sorts of families, all sorts of relationships and intimacies, diverse sexualities, friendships and acquaintanceships. The term 'personal' is also significant in denoting the centrality of the individual, yet avoiding the sense in which it can convey ideas of separateness, autonomy and the conceptual slide into individualization. So the term 'personal' allows for the role of agency and personal meanings, but also retains notions of connectedness and embeddedness in and with the social and the cultural.

Throughout this book – and especially in this conclusion – I am aware of the frequency with which I have alluded to threads, meshing and weaving or woven webs of relationships. Some of these images are deliberately evocative of the multi-dimensional life world, which is always difficult to capture in writing; but they are also terms which are not traditionally sociological – even if they are now entering the vocabulary (e.g. Griffiths, 1995). Borrowing visual terms from creative arts possibly reflects a lack of sufficiently sensitive or imaginative social 'scientific' terminology to capture the textures of personal life. But it may also be that it is important to develop a language of connectedness and depth if sociology is to become better equipped at encapsulating those qualities. Such language would be able to incorporate the intangible elements of connection and emotion. For example, deceased loved ones can be said not only to be remembered, but to leave traces through the lives of the living, exerting influences and changing lived experience. Or, in order to create networks of support, dormant or even unknown relationships can be (re)activated at critical moments in life or at times of migration. These slightly veiled terms can nudge existing understandings and meanings into different shapes and directions. But not only have I borrowed from imaginative terminologies, I have trespassed on other disciplines in my attempt to think differently about personal life. I have taken insights from anthropology, social history, law and (to a lesser extent) psychology. In so doing I have not tried to incorporate these other disciplines but rather to stretch the boundaries of sociology in different ways. Since sociology is a malleable form of knowing it has a flexible reach and considerable capacity to expand.

If a term is needed to capture the nature of this project it would be the 'connectedness thesis', which could stand in antithesis to the individualization thesis. Connectedness is not a normative concept and I am not arguing that connection is a human good, nor that it is invariably nourishing and inevitably desirable. On the contrary, I have highlighted some of the problems of connecting with and relating to others. The point about the idea, however, is that it sets the sociological imagination off on a different intellectual trajectory to the one initiated by the individualization thesis. With the latter, one is directed towards gathering information and evidence about fragmentation, differentiation, separation and autonomy. And it also becomes a mindset or inferential framework through which information is interpreted. This tendency needs to be counter-balanced by an awareness of connection, relationship, reciprocal emotion, entwinement, memory, history and so on. Connectedness as a mindset encourages enquiry about all kinds of sociality and seeks to understand how association remains both possible and desirable, as well as how it may take different shapes at different times. But this must not come across as trite, whimsical or contrary. This vision is closely related to my understanding of personal life as derived from the empirical research projects in which I have been involved. In other words, it is grounded sociologically speaking as well as poised to initiate a new intellectual direction.

The approach that I am advocating is also, in some ways, a response to the challenge set by Ulrich Beck (2002). As mentioned above, he argues that the family is now a 'zombie category'; in being so provocative he has sought to prod sociology into waking up from its 'drowsy fixation' with the nucleus of the family (Beck and Beck-Gernsheim, 1995: 147). He implies that as a field of enquiry the sociology of family life has become moribund and dull, quite incapable of grasping much of what is happening to family life and relationships. Beck may be right to acknowledge a lack of theoretical excitement in the field. Where once feminist work turned the whole concept of the family into a site of fruitful intellectual conflict, subsequent work settled into a pattern of empirical research which, in the main, sought to establish or modify those important insights and claims. So Giddens, Beck and Beck-Gernsheim have certainly caused a stir, and their work has, to a large extent, rushed in to fill the theoretical vacuum that they have identified. But what is really needed is an approach that goes beyond their limitations to offer both empirical grounding and a new theoretical orientation, thus initiating a new wave of research and thinking. It is here that the idea of the connectedness thesis comes in, along with the newly designated field of personal life.

Throughout this book I have stressed the significance of the personal and personal meanings as central to this approach. So I now pick up the final thread in my overall argument, which is an intellectual and ethical commitment to representing the everyday lives of ordinary people in the fullest and most nuanced ways possible. This has been a long-term goal of many sociologists, whether one relies on classical thinkers such as C. Wright Mills (1967, orig. 1959) and Alan Dawe (1970) or, later, Beverley Skeggs (1997). As Skeggs has perceptively stated in relation to her own problematic early attempts at analysing the complexities of the lives of working-class women:

> This led me at times to map my frameworks directly onto [women's] experiences without listening to or hearing what they were saying. [. . .] It was a product of my desperateness to understand the infinite number of things that were happening around me that led to this lapse in reflexivity. (1997: 31)

In this honest and self-critical account Skeggs points out how real people and their lives can become a kind of grist to a pre-existing theoretical mill. They are reduced to ciphers for a culturally and historically specific knowledge-building industry. Putting the argument against this tendency with quiet simplicity, Paul Johnson states: 'Most importantly, we need to do justice to the real lives of the individuals we study' (2005: 18). Arguably the excited reach of recent grand theorizing has not been aware of the wisdom of such a maxim and so presents the world as peopled with rather one-dimensional characters. It is precisely to broaden and deepen this limited view of personal relationships that I have raised many of the issues addressed above. Hence this book is my attempt to reconnect themes and reflections that have either been marginalized or become disconnected; in doing so, I have aimed to give ample space for the muddle and contradictions that go to make up relationships. I have striven to do this in a way that maps out a newly designated field of sociological enquiry, namely personal life.

Notes

Chapter 1   A Sociology of Personal Life

1   A possible exception was Ann Oakley's *The Sociology of Housework* (1974), a classic study that generated a huge debate and opened up a new field of enquiry.

2   Although much of the work that focuses on earlier periods tends to be historical, these studies can be said to have formed the foundation of sociological (and popular) thinking on family change over time (see Laslett, 1977, 2005; Shorter, 1976; Pollock, 1988, orig. 1983). Moreover, the debates within social history between the grand theorists and the more detailed empirical researchers mirrors very closely the same struggles in sociology.

3   As Peter Laslett (orig. 1965) asserted: 'It is not true that most of our ancestors lived in extended families. It is not true that industrialization brought the simple nuclear family with it. [. . .] It is not true that the elderly and the widowed ordinarily had their married children living with them, or that uncles, aunts, nephews and nieces were often to be found as resident relatives. It is not even true that the casualties of earlier, harder times, [. . .] could usually rely on their kin for continuing maintenance even though they did not live with them' (2005: 91).

4 Jean-Louis Flandrin (1979: 166) dated this growth somewhat earlier, suggesting that the Puritans in England in the second half of the sixteenth century were already speaking of true marriage as requiring a joining of hearts and a knitting of affections.

5 See Smart (2005a) for a discussion of the ways in which people will join in 'public' forms of decrying contemporary family life, while holding fast to it in their own lives.

6 But again here it is not entirely clear whether they mean that the traditional family must be abandoned or whether any and all types of family must be eschewed.

7 Notwithstanding the fact that their research offers a more complex picture than does Giddens; see also Mauthner, 2005.

Chapter 2   The Cultural Turn in the Sociology of Family Life

1 I shall not be pursuing a Bourdieusian analysis, however. Rather my approach is eclectic and seeks to rely on the theoretical and empirical work that has been attentive to questions of kinship and relationships. Moreover, as Elizabeth Silva (2005) has argued, Bourdieu's analysis of family life is deeply problematic.

2 As C. Wright Mills (orig. 1959) argued: 'The social scientist who spends his intellectual force on the details of small-scale milieux is not putting his work outside the political conflicts and forces of his time. He is, at least indirectly and in effect, "accepting" the framework of his society' (1967: 78).

3 Recall is not, of course, necessarily a conscious process: smells or revisiting places and old haunts can prompt memories unaided; the notion of memories 'flooding back' captures a sense of involuntariness.

4 I use the male form advisedly here because this type of individual was conceived of in almost exclusively masculine terms.

5 It is also worth noting that Finch finds some of the historical statements that surround the English loathing of kinship and family ties to be excessive. There is clearly a debate about the peculiarity of 'the English' and their apparent desire to diminish kinship obligations and to divest themselves of relatives. On the one hand there is the cliché that 'blood is thicker than water', but on the other is the view that 'one can choose one's friends, but not one's relatives', suggesting that kin are foist upon one whereas natural inclination would lead to different bonds.

Chapter 3   Emotions, Love and the Problem of Commitment

1 'Gay and Lesbian "Marriage": An Exploration of the Meanings and Significance of Legitimating Same Sex Relationships' (ESRC, RES-000230418). For the final report of this project, see http://www. ESRC.ac.uk.

2 Sayer is slightly overstating his criticism of sociology's lack of attention to 'morality' here. After all, feminist sociology was much taken up by this issue throughout the 1990s.

3 In this study we interviewed couples as pairs when possible. We asked them to tell us how they got together but also to explain why they wanted a ceremony/marriage and how this affected their relationship with each other and with wider friends and family. For full accounts of the methods, see Shipman and Smart, 2007. For a discussion of the problems of eliciting accounts in interview settings, see Smart, 2006.

Chapter 4   Connections, Threads and Cultures of Tradition

1 The concept of the 'relational self' (Meyers, ed., 1997; Flax, 1990) accommodates this dichotomy, as discussed later in this chapter.

2 The interview was part of the ESRC Research Group project 'Care, Values and the Future of Welfare' (known as CAVA), Leeds University 1999–2004, M564281001. See http://www.ESRC.ac.uk and Smart, 2005a and b. Dr Bren Neale worked with me on the study and we shared the interviews between us.

3 This small study was funded by the ESRC as part of an extension of CAVA (see preceding note). Dr Shelley Budgeon worked with me on the study and we shared the interviews between us.

4 The *Empire Windrush* was the boat that brought one of the first groups of Caribbean migrant workers to Britain in 1948. It has come to symbolize a key moment in the history of multi-cultural Britain as well as the experiences of those first migrants.

5 It must be emphasized that family story-telling may not be about imparting admirable moral qualities; the stories might equally be about getting away with abuse, violence or any anti-social activity.

6 As Helen pointed out: 'Well the thing is West Indians have such traditional English names. His brother is Charles. He's called Andrew. I mean could you come up with a more English name than that?'

7 I noted at the start that these were predominantly professional families and so the ability to turn what might for some be a cultural deficit into cultural capital is undoubtedly related to their class position and I am not suggesting that it is always possible or inevitable that this happens.

8 As Mavis put it: 'They are aware, if you ask them – I mean I have said this, would you consider yourselves more American or British? They both consider themselves British. They know they are Jewish. I don't know if they would say it though, if they would actually in describing themselves use, use that. But it's been a very mixed background because you know we've gone back and forth between the countries.'

9 I could for example have stressed the stories of rejection by grandparents; one of them even refused to acknowledge the existence of a mixed-race grandchild.

Chapter 5   Secrets and Lies

1 For example, search 'family' and 'secret' on any newspaper website and thousands of articles pop up, ranging from those invoking celebrities to sad stories about ordinary people; the lure of family secrets is certainly not exclusively linked to a prurient interest in the rich and famous. Among the innumerable personal accounts, see that by Colin Harris in *The Guardian*, 11 February 2006 (Family Section, page 3). The article was featured under the summary: 'As a child Colin Harris was fond of his Uncle Bill. A close family friend, Bill bought him books and taught him Scrabble. It was only years later he realised why they had so much in common.'

2 For example the BBC website http://www.bbc.co.uk/history/ familyhistory has 13 pages listing specific items under the heading 'Family Secrets'. One was at one stage flagged in these terms: 'Find out how to discover the skeletons and scandals in your ancestors' closets'.

3 For example, the BBC television documentary series *Who Do You Think You Are?*, which began in 2004, traces the family backgrounds of various celebrities. In some cases it has uncovered some very painful secrets (or at least buried knowledge), causing distress and anguish. However, the general theme of the programmes is that it is a 'good thing' to know the truth about the past, no matter how painful.

4 This meant that I never knew I had a maternal uncle, nor that he had children living in England.

5 Indeed she was one of those who flirted with the Fascist Party of Oswald Mosley before the war.

6 Klein (2005) outlines the irregular nature of much working-class domestic life in Liverpool, Birmingham and Manchester at this time. Although she was studying life in cities (through records kept on police families in those cities) her research reveals just how much separation went on, as well as how many men and women repartnered while still being legally married. Even the police who were supposed to be 'respectable' seemed to behave in ways which certainly did not fit the Victorian middle-class ideal.

7 It is vital to remember that women could earn very little in the mainstream labour market. Pension provision for unsupported women, even after the reforms of 1948, amounted to penury; it was based on a National Insurance contribution record of forty years for a full pension. So few women could qualify.

8 Wodehouse was a prolific author whose novels about Bertie Wooster, a foppish, wealthy, accident-prone gentleman, and his valet Jeeves humorously represent the life style of the leisured upper classes in England during the 1920s and 1930s. The names of the characters themselves conjure up an image of the era, e.g. Augustus Fink-Nottle, nicknamed 'Gussie', Hildebrand Glossop, 'Tuppy'; Reginald Herring, 'Kipper'.

9 There are now countless published biographies, novels and especially family sagas which start in penury around the time of the First World War (often in the North of England) and end in London in contemporary times. Examples include William Woodruff's *The Road to Nab End: A Lancashire Childhood* (2002, orig. 1993 as *Billy Boy*), Gilda O'Neill's *My East End* (1999), Margaret Forster's *Diary of an Ordinary Woman* (2003) and even Melvyn Bragg's *The Soldier's Return* (1999).

10 For details of this study, see chapter 4, n. 2 above.

11 Although this was not a position supported by the Church of England.

12 *Re F* [1993] 1 FLR 598.

13 There are now well over 550,000 websites advertising paternity testing, alongside discussions about men's need to have certainty about paternity.

14 *In Re D (A Child Appearing by her Guardian ad litem (Respondent)* [2005] UKHL 33.

Chapter 6   Families we Live with

1 The study entitled 'Post-divorce Childhoods: Perspectives from Children' was carried out with Dr Bren Neale and was funded by the Nuffield Foundation. The main findings are reported in Smart, Neale and Wade, 2001.

2 'Enduring Families: Children's Long Term Reflections on Post-divorce Family Life' (ESRC, R00239248) was carried out with Dr Bren Neale as Principal Investigator, and Dr Jennifer Flowerdew as research officer. See http://www.ESRC.ac.uk and Smart, 2006.

3 Of course adults were often aware of the normative requirement for loyalty.

4 We gave careful consideration to giving children back their interview transcripts so that they could comment on them or change things. However in the end we did not do this for several reasons. The first was that very young children would have found the volume and dryness of the texts difficult to handle, and the second was that they would have inevitably needed their parents' help if they were young. This would have meant that everything the children told us would have become known to their parents. Even with older children we felt that this was very likely to happen. So the practice of allowing interviewees to have their transcripts back gave way to the ethical considerations of confidentiality.

5 Maja was one of the grandparents interviewed as part of our ESRC-funded study entitled 'Continuity and Change in Parent-Child Relations over Three Generations', led by Dr Amanda Wade (R000239523). Where possible, we interviewed three generations in different families in order to explore how ideas and practices around child-raising have changed.

6 ESRC Research Group: 'Care, Values and the Future of Welfare (CAVA): The Transnational Kinship Study', M564281001, which I led with Jennifer Mason and Louise Ackers. In this study we interviewed two generations of families in Pakistani, Indian and Irish families in Bradford and Leeds in 2002–3. For details, see Smart and Shipman, 2004.

7 See n. 2 above.

8 This study, funded by the Joseph Rowntree Foundation, involved interviewing primary school children in four very different schools in

the North of England to explore their experiences of family break-down and change. For full details, see Wade and Smart, 2002.

9 Feminist work in the 1970s and 1980s challenged this view, but the focus then was particularly on how problematic families were for women. Now it seems we can recognize that toxic relationships can affect everybody, especially children.

Chapter 7   Possessions, Things and Relationality

1 This was part of the ESRC Research Group on 'Care, Values and the Future of Welfare' (CAVA, M564281001; see chapter 4, n. 2 above). See also Smart and Shipman, 2004.

2 These quotations also come from the transnational families project; see preceding note.

3 For details of this project, see chapter 3, n. 1 above. See also http://www.socialsciences.manchester.ac.uk/morgancentre; Shipman and Smart, 2007.

4 This does seem a particularly interesting slip of the tongue.

References

Adie, K. (2005) *Nobody's Child*, London: Hodder and Stoughton

Ahmed, S. (2000) *Strange Encounters: Embodied Others in Post-Coloniality*, London: Routledge

Allan, G. (1985) *Family Life: Domestic Roles and Social Organization*, Oxford: Blackwell

Allan, G. (1989) *Friendship: Developing a Sociological Perspective*, Hemel Hempstead: Harvester Wheatsheaf

Allan, G. (1996) *Kinship and Friendship in Modern Britain*, Oxford: Oxford University Press

Allan, G., and Crow, G. (1989) (eds) *Home and Family: Creating the Domestic Sphere*, Basingstoke: Macmillan

Andrews, M., Sclater, S. D., Squire, C., and Treacher, A. (2000) (eds) *Lines of Narrative*, London: Routledge

Ariès, P. (1962, French orig. 1960) *Centuries of Childhood*, London: Cape

Bailey, J. (2003) *Unquiet Lives: Marriage and Marriage Breakdown in England, 1660–1800*, Cambridge: Cambridge University Press

Barbalet, J. (1998) *Emotion, Social Theory, and Social Structure: A Macrosociological Approach*, Cambridge: Cambridge University Press

Barbalet, J. (ed.) (2002) *Emotions and Sociology*, Oxford: Blackwell

Barrett, M. (1992) 'Words and Things: Materialism and Method in Contemporary Feminist Analysis', in M. Barrett and A. Phillips (eds) *Destabilizing Theory*, Cambridge: Polity

Barrett, M., and McIntosh, M. (1982) *The Anti-Social Family*, London: Verso

Barry, K. (1979) *Female Sexual Slavery*, New York: New York University Press

Bauman, Z. (2001) *The Individualized Society*, Cambridge: Polity

Bauman, Z. (2003) *Liquid Love*, Cambridge: Polity

Bauman, Z. (2005) *Liquid Life*, Cambridge: Polity

Beauvoir, S. de (1972, French orig. 1949) *The Second Sex*, Harmondsworth: Penguin

Beck, U. (1992) *Risk Society: Towards a New Modernity*, London: Sage

Beck, U., and Beck-Gernsheim, E. (1995) *The Normal Chaos of Love*, Cambridge: Polity

Beck, U., and Beck-Gernsheim, E. (2002) *Individualization*, London: Sage

Beck-Gernsheim, E. (2002) *Reinventing the Family: In Search of New Lifestyles*, Cambridge: Polity

Bendelow, G., and Williams, S. (eds) (1998) *Emotions in Social Life*, London: Routledge

Bengtson, V., Biblarz, T., and Roberts, R. (2002) *How Families Still Matter*, Cambridge: Cambridge University Press

Bennet, O. (2001) *Cultural Pessimism: Narratives of Decline in the Postmodern World*, Edinburgh: Edinburgh University Press

Berger, B., and Berger, P. (1983) *The War over the Family: Capturing the Middle Ground*, Harmondsworth: Pelican Books

Berger, J. (1972) *Ways of Seeing*, Harmondsworth: Penguin

Bernard, J. (1976) *The Future of Marriage*, Harmondsworth: Penguin

Bertaux, D., and Thompson, P. (eds) (2005) *Between Generations: Family Models, Myths and Memories*, London: Transaction Publishers

Blankenhorn, D., Bayme, S., and Elshtain, J. B. (eds) (1990) *Rebuilding the Nest: A New Commitment to the American Family*, Milwaukee: Family Service America

Bloch, C. (2002) 'Managing the Emotions of Competition and Recognition in Academia', in J. Barbalet (ed.) *Emotions and Sociology*, Oxford: Blackwell

Blokland, T. (2005) 'Memory Magic: How a Working-Class Neighbourhood Became an Imagined Community and Class Started to Matter when it Lost its Base', in F. Devine et al. (eds) *Rethinking Class*, Basingstoke: Palgrave Macmillan

Bochner, A. P. (2001) 'Narrative's Virtues', *Qualitative Inquiry*, 7 (2): 131–57

Bourdieu, P. (1977) *Outline of a Theory of Practice*, Cambridge: Cambridge University Press

Bowlby, R. (2001) *Carried Away: The Invention of Modern Shopping*, New York: Columbia University Press

Bowlby, S., Gregory, S., and McKie, L. (1997) ' "Doing Home": Patriarchy, Caring and Space', *Women's Studies International Forum*, 20 (3): 343–4

Bradley, H., and Fenton, S. (1999) 'Reconciling Culture and Economy: Ways Forward in the Analysis of Ethnicity and Gender', in L. Ray and A. Sayer (eds) *Culture and Economy after the Cultural Turn*, London: Sage

Brannen, J., and Moss, P. (1991) *Managing Mothers*, London: Unwin Hyman

Brannen, J., and Nilsen, A. (2005) 'Individualisation, Choice and Structure: A Discussion of Current Trends in Sociological Analysis', *Sociological Review*, 53 (3): 412–28

Brannen, J., Moss, P., and Mooney, A. (2004) *Working and Caring over the Twentieth Century*, Basingstoke: Palgrave Macmillan

Brison, S. J. (1997) 'Outliving Oneself: Trauma, Memory and Personal Identity', in D. T. Meyers (ed.) *Feminists Rethink the Self*, Boulder, Colo., and Oxford: Westview Press

Burgoyne, C. (1990) 'Money in Marriage: How Patterns of Allocation both Reflect and Conceal Power', *Sociological Review*, 38 (4): 634–65

Burgoyne, C., and Morison, V. (1997) 'Money in Remarriage: Keeping Things Simple – and Separate', *Sociological Review*, 45 (3): 363–95

Burgoyne, C., Clarke, V., Reibstein, J., and Edmunds, A. (2006) ' "All my worldly goods I share with you"? Managing Money at the Transition to Heterosexual Marriage', *Sociological Review*, 54 (4): 619–37

Burkitt, I. (1997) 'Social Relationships and Emotions', *Sociology*, 31 (1): 37–55

Burkitt, I. (2002) 'Complex Emotions: Relations, Feelings and Images in Emotional Experience', in J. Barbalet (ed.) *Emotions and Sociology*, Oxford: Blackwell

Carling, A., Duncan, S., and Edwards, R. (2002) (eds) *Analysing Families: Morality and Rationality in Policy and Practice*, London: Routledge

Carsten, J. (2000) '"Knowing where you've come from": Ruptures and Continuities of Time and Kinship in Narratives of Adoption', *Journal of the Royal Anthropological Institute*, 6: 687–703

Carsten, J. (2004) *After Kinship*, Cambridge: Cambridge University Press

Chapman, D. (1955) *The Home and Social Status*, London: Routledge and Kegan Paul

Chapman, T., and Hockey, J. (eds) (1999) *Ideal Homes? Social Change and Domestic Life*, London: Routledge

Charles, N., and Kerr, M. (1988) *Women, Food and Families*, Manchester: Manchester University Press

Comer, L. (1974) *Wedlocked Women*, Leeds: Feminist Books

Connerton, P. (1994, orig. 1989) *How Societies Remember*, Cambridge: Cambridge University Press

Corden, A., and Sainsbury, R. (2006) *Using Verbatim Quotations in Reporting Qualitative Social Research: Researchers' Views*, Report to the ESRC, York: University of York, Social Policy Research Unit

Corrigan, P. (1997) *The Sociology of Consumption*, London: Sage

Craib, I. (1994) *The Importance of Disappointment*, London: Routledge

Crompton, R. (2006) 'Class and Family', *Sociological Review*, 54 (4): 658–77

Crossley, N. (1998) 'Emotion and Communicative Action: Habermas, Linguistic Philosophy and Existentialism', in G. Bendelow and S. Williams (eds) *Emotions in Social Life*, London: Routledge

Crow, G. (2002) 'Families, Moralities, Rationalities and Social Change', in A. Carling, S. Duncan and R. Edwards (eds) *Analysing Families*, London: Routledge

Davidoff, L., and Hall, C. (1987) *Family Fortunes*, London: Hutchinson

Davidoff, L., Doolittle, M., Fink, J., and Holden, K. (1999) *The Family Story: Blood, Contract and Intimacy, 1830–1960*, London: Longman

Dawe, A. (1970) 'The Two Sociologies', *British Journal of Sociology*, 21 (2): 207–18

Delphy, C., and Leonard, D. (1992) *Familiar Exploitation*, Cambridge: Polity

Dench, G. (1997) *Rewriting the Sexual Contract*, London: Institute of Community Studies

Dennis, N., and Erdos, G. (1993) *Families without Fatherhood*, London: Institute of Economic Affairs, Choice in Welfare Series no. 12

Denzin, N. (1984) *On Understanding Emotions*, San Francisco: Jossey-Bass

DeVault, M. L. (1994) *Feeding the Family*, Chicago and London: University of Chicago Press

Devine, F. (1989) 'Privatised Families and their Homes', in G. Allan and G. Crow (eds) *Home and Family: Creating the Domestic Sphere*, Basingstoke: Macmillan

Devine, F., and Savage, M. (2005) 'The Cultural Turn, Sociology and Class Analysis', in Devine et al. (eds) *Rethinking Class: Culture, Identities and Lifestyle*, Basingstoke: Palgrave Macmillan

Devine, F., Savage, M., Scott, J., and Crompton, R. (2005) (eds) *Rethinking Class: Culture, Identities and Lifestyle*, Basingstoke: Palgrave Macmillan

Dobash, R. E., and Dobash, R. (1980) *Violence against Wives*, Somerset: Open Books

Donovan, C. (2006) 'Genetics, Fathers and Families: Exploring the Implications of Changing the Law in Favour of Identifying Sperm Donors', *Social & Legal Studies*, 15 (4): 494–510

Duncan, S., Barlow, A., and James, G. (2005) 'Why Don't They Marry?: Cohabitation, Commitment and DIY Marriage', *Child and Family Law Quarterly*, 17 (3): 383–98

Duncan, S., and Smith, D. (2006) 'Individualisation versus the Geography of "new" Families', *Twenty First Century Society*, 1 (2): 167–89

Duncombe, J., and Marsden, D. (1993) 'Love and Intimacy: The Gender Division of Emotion and "Emotion Work"', *Sociology*, 27 (2): 221–41

Duncombe, J., and Marsden, D. (1998) ' "Stepford Wives" and "Hollow Men"?: Doing Emotion Work, Doing Gender and "Authenticity" in Intimate Heterosexual Relationships', in G. Bendelow and S. Williams (eds) *Emotions in Social Life*, London: Routledge

Dupuis, A., and Thorns, D. C. (1998) 'Home, Home Ownership and the Search for Ontological Security', *Sociological Review*, 46 (1): 24–47

Edwards, J. (2000) *Born and Bred*, Oxford: Oxford University Press

Edwards, J., and Strathern, M. (2000) 'Including our Own', in J. Carsten (ed.) *Cultures of Relatedness: New Approaches to the Study of Kinship*, Cambridge: Cambridge University Press

Edwards, S. (1989) *Policing 'Domestic' Violence: Women, the Law and the State*, London: Sage

Eekelaar, J., and Maclean, M. (2004) 'Marriage and the Moral Bases of Personal Relationships', *Journal of Law and Society*, 31 (4): 510–38

Ehrenreich, B. (1983) *The Hearts of Men*, London: Pluto Press

Elder, G. H., Jr. (1994) 'Time, Human Agency, and Social Change: Perspectives on the Life Course', *Social Psychology Quarterly*, 57: 4–15

Elias, N. (2000, German orig. 1939) *The Civilizing Process*, Oxford: Blackwell

Etzioni, A. (1993) *Parenting Deficit*, London: Demos

Evans, M. (2003) *Love: An Unromantic Discussion*, Cambridge: Polity

Finch, J. (1989) *Family Obligations and Social Change*, Cambridge: Polity

Finch, J., and Groves, D. (1983) (eds), *A Labour of Love: Women, Work and Caring*, London: Routledge and Kegan Paul

Finch, J., and Hayes, L. (1994) 'Inheritance, Death and the Concept of the Home', *Sociology*, 28 (2): 417–33

Finch, J., and Mason, J. (1993) *Negotiating Family Responsibilities*, London: Tavistock/Routledge

Finch, J., and Mason, J. (2000) *Passing On: Kinship and Inheritance in England*, London: Routledge

Finch, J., and Summerfield, P. (1991) 'Social Reconstruction and the Emergence of Companionate Marriage, 1945–1959', in D. Clark (ed.) *Marriage, Domestic Life and Social Change*, London: Routledge

Fineman, S. (ed.) (2000) *Emotion in Organizations*, London: Sage

Fiske, A. P. (1991) *Structures of Social Life*, New York: Free Press

Flandrin, J.-L. (1979) *Families in Former Times*, Cambridge: Cambridge University Press

Flax, J. (1990) *Thinking Fragments*, Berkeley: University of California Press

Fletcher, R. (1966, orig. 1962) *The Family and Marriage in Britain*, Harmondsworth: Penguin

Forster, M. (2000) *The Memory Box*, Harmondsworth: Penguin

Fortin, J. (1994) '*Re F*: "The Gooseberry Bush Approach"', *Modern Law Review*, 57 (2): 296–307

Foucault, M. (1979, French orig. 1976) *The History of Sexuality, Volume 1*, London: Allen Lane

Frankenberg, R. (1957) *Village on the Border*, London: Cohen and West

Freeman, T., and Richards, M. (2006) 'DNA Testing and Kinship: Paternity, Genealogy and the Search for the "Truth" of our Genetic Origins', in F. Ebtehaj, B. Lindley and M. Richards (eds) *Kin Matters*, Oxford: Hart Publishing

Furedi, F. (2004) *Therapy Culture: Cultivating Vulnerability in an Uncertain Age*, London: Routledge

Gavron, H. (1983) *The Captive Wife*, London: Routledge and Kegan Paul

Geertz, C. (1973) *The Interpretation of Cultures: Selected Essays*, New York: Basic Books

Geertz, C. (2000, orig. 1985) *Local Knowledge: Further Essays in Interpretive Anthropology*, New York: Basic Books

Gergen, K. (1994) *Realities and Relationships: Soundings in Social Construction*, Cambridge, Mass.: Harvard University Press

Giddens, A. (1992) *The Transformation of Intimacy*, Cambridge: Polity

Gill, D. (1977) *Illegitimacy, Sexuality and the Status of Women*, Oxford: Blackwell

Gillis, J. (1996) *A World of their Own Making: Myth, Ritual, and the Quest for Family Values*, Cambridge, Mass.: Harvard University Press

Gillis, J. (2004) 'Gathering Together', in A. Etzioni and J. Bloom (eds) *We Are What We Celebrate: Understanding Holidays and Rituals*, New York: New York University Press

Glendinning, C., and Millar, J. (1987) *Women and Poverty in Britain*, Brighton: Wheatsheaf

Goldthorpe, J. H., Lockwood, D., Bechhofer, F., and Platt, J. (1969) *The Affluent Worker in the Class Structure*, Cambridge: Cambridge University Press

Goudsblom, J., and Mennell, S. (eds) (1998) *The Norbert Elias Reader*, Oxford: Blackwell

Graham, H. (1983) 'Caring: A Labour of Love', in J. Finch and D. Groves (eds) *A Labour of Love: Women, Work and Caring*, London: Routledge and Kegan Paul

Griffiths, M. (1995) *Feminisms and the Self: The Web of Identity*, London: Routledge

Gross, N. (2005) 'The Detraditionalization of Intimacy Reconsidered', *Sociological Theory*, 23 (3): 286–311

Gurney, C. (1997) '". . . Half of me was satisfied": Making Sense of Home through Episodic Ethnographies', *Women's Studies International Forum*, 20 (3): 373–86

Hamilton, C. (1981, orig. 1909) *Marriage as a Trade*, London: The Women's Press

Hanmer, J., Griffiths, S., and Jerwood, D. (1999) *Arresting Evidence: Domestic Violence and Repeat Victimisation*, London: Home Office Policing and Reducing Crime Unit

Hazleden, R. (2004) 'The Pathology of Love in Contemporary Relationship Manuals', *Sociological Review*, 52 (2): 201–17

Heaphy, B., Weeks, J., and Donovan, C. (1999) 'Sex, Money and the Kitchen Sink: Power in Same-Sex Couple Relationships', in

J. Seymour and P. Bagguley (eds) *Relating Intimacies: Power and Resistance*, Basingstoke: Macmillan

Hecht, A. (2001) 'Home Sweet Home: Tangible Memories of an Uprooted Childhood', in D. Miller (ed.) *Home Possessions*, Oxford: Berg

Hester, M. (2000) *Making an Impact: Children and Domestic Violence*, London: Jessica Kingsley

Hochschild, A. R. (1975) 'The Sociology of Feeling and Emotion: Selected Possibilities', in M. Millman and R. Moss Kanter (eds) *Another Voice*, New York: Anchor Books

Hochschild, A. R. (2003) *The Managed Heart*, Berkeley: University of California Press

Hoffman, E. (2005) *After Such Knowledge*, London: Vintage

Hurdley, R. (2006) 'Dismantling Mantelpieces: Narrating Identities and Materializing Culture in the Home', *Sociology*, 40 (4): 717–33

Jackson, E. (2001) *Regulating Reproduction: Law, Technology and Autonomy*, Oxford: Hart Publishing

Jackson, S. (1993) 'Even Sociologists Fall in Love: An Exploration in the Sociology of Emotions', *Sociology*, 27 (2): 201–20

Jamieson, L. (1998) *Intimacy: Personal Relationships in Modern Societies*, Cambridge: Polity

Jamieson, L. (1999) 'Intimacy Transformed?: A Critical Look at the "Pure Relationship"', *Sociology*, 33 (3): 477–94

Jamieson, L., Anderson, M., McCrome, D., Bechhofer, F., Stewart, R., and Li, Y. (2002) 'Cohabitation and Commitment: Partnership Plans of Young Men and Women', *Sociological Review*, 50 (3): 356–77

Jeffreys, S. (1985) *The Spinster and her Enemies*, London: Pandora

Johnson, P. (2005) *Love, Heterosexuality and Society*, London: Routledge

Kemmer, D. (2000) 'Tradition and Change in Domestic Roles and Food Preparation', *Sociology*, 34 (2): 323–33

Kemmer, D., Anderson, A. S., and Marshall, D. W. (1998) 'Living Together and Eating Together: Changes in Food Choice and Eating Habits during the Transition from Single to Married/Cohabiting', *Sociological Review*, 46 (1): 49–72

Kendell, K. (2006) 'The Right to Marry and the San Francisco Experience', *Family Court Review*, 44 (1): 33–44

Klein, J. (2005) 'Irregular Marriages: Unorthodox Working-Class Domestic Life in Liverpool, Birmingham, and Manchester 1900–1939', *Journal of Family History*, 30 (2): 210–29

Komter, A. (2001) 'Heirlooms, Nikes and Bribes: Towards a Sociology of Things', *Sociology*, 35 (1): 59–75

Kuhn, A. (1995) *Family Secrets: Acts of Memory and Imagination*, London: Verso

Laing, R. D. (1969) *The Divided Self*, Harmondsworth: Penguin

Langford, W. (1999) *Revolutions of the Heart*, London: Routledge

Laslett, P. (1977) *Family Life and Illicit Love in Earlier Generations*, Cambridge: Cambridge University Press

Laslett, P. (2005, orig. 1965) *The World We Have Lost – Further Explored*, London: Routledge

Lewis, J. (2001) *The End of Marriage?*, Cheltenham: Edward Elgar

Lewis, J. (2005) 'Perceptions of Risk in Intimate Relationships: The Implications for Social Provision', *Journal of Social Policy*, 35 (1): 39–57

Lieberman, S. (1979) 'A Transgenerational Theory', *Journal of Family Therapy*, 1 (3): 347–60

Lupton, D. (1998) *The Emotional Self*, London: Sage

Macfarlane, A. (1979) *The Origins of English Individualism: The Family, Property and Social Transition*, Cambridge: Cambridge University Press

Mallett, S. (2004) 'Understanding Home: A Critical Review of the Literature', *Sociological Review*, 52 (1): 62–89

Mansfield, P., and Collard, J. (1988) *The Beginning of the Rest of your Life?*, Basingstoke: Macmillan

Marcoux, J.-S. (2001) 'The Refurbishment of Memory', in D. Miller (ed.) *Home Possessions*, Oxford: Berg

Marwick, A. (1971) *The Explosion of British Society 1914–70*, London: Macmillan

Marwick, A. (1982) *British Society since 1945*, Harmondsworth: Penguin

Mason, J. (1989) 'Reconstructing the Public and the Private: The Home and Marriage in Later Life', in G. Allan and G. Crow (eds) *Home and Family: Creating the Domestic Sphere*, Basingstoke: Macmillan

Mason, J. (1996) 'Gender, Care and Sensibility in Family and Kin Relationships', in J. Holland and L. Atkins (eds) *Sex, Sensibility and the Gendered Body*, Basingstoke: Macmillan

Mason, J. (2002, orig. 1996) *Qualitative Researching*, London: Sage

Mason, J. (2004) 'Personal Narratives, Relational Selves: Residential Histories in the Living and Telling', *Sociological Review*, 52 (2): 162–79

Mauthner, M. (2005) *Sistering: Power and Change in Female Relationships*, Basingstoke: Palgrave Macmillan

May, M. (1978) 'Violence in the Family: An Historical Perspective', in J. P. Marton (ed.) *Violence in the Family*, Chichester: John Wiley

McGregor, O. R. (1957) *Divorce in England*, London: Heinemann

McRobbie, A. (1991) *Feminism and Youth Culture*, Basingstoke: Macmillan

Mead, G. H. (1967, orig. 1934) *Mind, Self, and Society*, Chicago: University of Chicago Press

Mendus, S. (2000) *Feminism and Emotion: Readings in Moral and Political Philosophy*, Basingstoke: Macmillan

Merleau-Ponty, M. (1962, French orig. 1945) *Phenomenology of Perception*, London: Routledge and Kegan Paul

Meyers, D. T. (1997) (ed.) *Feminists Rethink the Self*, Boulder, Colo., and Oxford: Westview Press

Miller, D. (1998) (ed.) *Material Cultures: Why Some Things Matter*, London: UCL Press

Miller, D. (2001) (ed.) *Home Possessions*, Oxford: Berg

Mills, C. W. (1940) 'Situated Actions and Vocabularies of Motive', *American Sociological Review*, 5 (6): 904–13

Mills, C. W. (1967, orig. 1959) *The Sociological Imagination*, Oxford: Oxford University Press

Misztal, B. (2003) *Theories of Social Remembering*, Buckingham: Open University Press

Mitchell, J. (2003) *Siblings*, Cambridge: Polity

Mitchell, W., and Green, E. (2002) ' "I don't know what I'd do without our Mam": Motherhood, Identity and Support Networks', *Sociological Review*, 50 (1): 1–22

Morgan, D. (1996) *Family Connections*, Cambridge: Polity

Morgan, P. (1995) *Farewell to the Family?*, London: Institute of Economic Affairs, Choice in Welfare Series no. 21

Morgan, P. (2000) *Marriage-Lite: The Rise of Cohabitation and its Consequences*, London: Institute for the Study of Civil Society

Murcott, A. (1983) *The Sociology of Food and Eating*, Aldershot: Gower

Murcott, A. (1997) 'Family Meals – A Thing of the Past?', in P. Caplan (ed.) *Food, Health and Identity*, London: Routledge

Nyman, C. (2003) 'The Social Nature of Money: Meanings of Money in Swedish Families', *Women's Studies International Forum*, 26 (1): 79–94

Oakley, A. (1974) *The Sociology of Housework*, Oxford: Martin Robertson

Pahl, J. (1980) 'Patterns of Money Management within Marriage', *Journal of Social Policy*, 9 (3): 313–35

Pahl, J. (1989) *Money and Marriage*, Basingstoke: Macmillan

Pahl, J. (1990) 'Household Spending, Personal Spending and the Control of Money in Marriage', *Sociology*, 24 (1): 119–38

Pahl, J., and Vogler, C. (1994) 'Money, Power and Inequality within Marriage', *Sociological Review*, 42 (2): 263–88

Pahl, R. (2000) *On Friendship*, Cambridge: Polity

Pahl, R., and Pevalin, D. (2005) 'Between Family and Friends: A Longitudinal Study of Friendship Choice', *British Journal of Sociology*, 56 (3): 433–50

Pahl, R., and Spencer, L. (2004) 'Personal Communities: Not Simply Families of "Fate" or "Choice"', *Current Sociology*, 52 (2): 199–221

Parsons, T., and Bales, R. (1955) *Family, Socialization and Interaction Process*, New York: Free Press

Pink, S. (2004) *Home Truths: Gender, Domestic Objects and Everyday Life*, Oxford: Berg

Pollock, L. A. (1988, orig. 1983) *Forgotten Children: Parent-child Relations from 1500 to 1900*, Cambridge: Cambridge University Press

Popenoe, D. (1993) 'American Family Decline, 1960–1990: A Review and Appraisal', *Journal of Marriage and the Family*, 55 (August): 527–55

Radstone, S. (2000) 'Working with Memory: An Introduction', in S. Radstone (ed.) *Memory and Methodology*, Oxford: Berg

Radway, J. (1984) *Reading the Romance*, London: University of North Carolina Press

Rapport, N., and Dawson, A. (1998) *Migrants of Identity: Perceptions of Home in a World of Movement*, Oxford: Berg

Ray, L., and Sayer, A. (1999) (eds) *Culture and Economy after the Cultural Turn*, London: Sage

Ribbens McCarthy, J., and Edwards, R. (2002) 'The Individual in Public and Private: The Significance of Mothers and Children', in A. Carling, S. Duncan and R. Edwards (eds) *Analysing Families: Morality and Rationality in Policy and Practice*, London: Routledge

Ribbens McCarthy, J., Edwards, R., and Gillies, V. (2003) *Making Families: Moral Tales of Parenting and Step-parenting*, Durham: SociologyPress

Richardson, D. (1996) *Theorising Heterosexuality*, Buckingham: Open University Press

Riley, D. (1983) *War in the Nursery: Theories of the Child and Mother*, London: Virago

Rose, J. (1987) *For the Sake of the Children*, London: Hodder and Stoughton

Rose, N. (1991) *Governing the Soul: The Shaping of the Private Self*, London: Routledge

Roseneil, S. (1995) 'The Coming of Age of Feminist Sociology: Some Issues of Theory and Practice for the Next Twenty Years', *British Journal of Sociology*, 26 (2): 191–203

Roseneil, S., and Budgeon, S. (2004) 'Beyond the Conventional Family: Intimacy, Care and Community in the 21st Century', *Current Sociology*, 52 (2): 135–59

Rosser, C., and Harris, C. (1983) *The Family and Social Change*, London: Routledge and Kegan Paul

Royal Commission on Marriage and Divorce, 1951–55, Report (1956) London: HMSO, Cmd. 9678

Russell, D. (1984) *Sexual Exploitation*, London: Sage

Rustin, M. (2000) 'Reflections on the Biographical Turn in Social Science', in P. Chamberlayne, J. Bornat and T. Wengraf (eds) *The Turn to Biographical Methods in Social Science*, London: Routledge

Sartre, J.-P. (1993, French orig. 1939) *The Emotions: Outline of a Theory*, New York: Citadel

Saunders, P. (1990) *A Nation of Home Owners*, London: Unwin-Hyman

Savage, M., Warde, A., and Devine, F. (2005) 'Capitals, Assets and Resources: Some Critical Issues', *British Journal of Sociology*, 56 (1): 31–47

Sayer, A. (2000) *Realism and Social Science*, London: Sage

Sayer, A. (2005) *The Moral Significance of Class*, Cambridge: Cambridge University Press

Seale, C. (2000) 'Resurrective Practice and Narrative', in M. Andrews, S. D. Sclater, C. Squire and A. Treacher (eds) *Lines of Narrative*, London: Routledge

Shaw, A. (2006, orig. 2000), *Kinship and Continuity: Pakistani Families in Britain*, London: Routledge; and Amsterdam: Harwood Academic Publishers

Shaw, A. (forthcoming) *Negotiating Risk: British Pakistani Experiences of Genetics*, Oxford: Berghahn

Sheldon, S. (2005) 'Reproductive Technologies and the Legal Determination of Fatherhood', *Feminist Legal Studies*, 13: 349–62

Shields, S. A. (2002) *Speaking from the Heart: Gender and the Social Meaning of Emotion*, Cambridge: Cambridge University Press

Shilling, C. (2002) 'The Two Traditions in the Sociology of Emotions', in J. Barbalet (ed.) *Emotions and Sociology*, Oxford: Blackwell

Shipman, B., and Smart, C. (2007) ' "It's Made a Huge Difference": Recognition, Rights and the Personal Significance of Civil Partnership', *Sociological Research Online*, 12 (1), 31 January

Shorter, E. (1976) *The Making of the Modern Family*, London: Collins

Silva, E. B. (1999) 'Transforming Housewifery: Practices, Dispositions and Technologies', in E. B. Silva and C. Smart (eds) *The New Family?*, London: Sage

Silva, E. B. (2005) 'Gender, Home and Family in Cultural Capital Theory', *British Journal of Sociology*, 56 (1): 83–103

Silva, E. B. and Smart, C. (1999) (eds) *The New Family?*, London: Sage

Skeggs, B. (1997) *Formations of Class and Gender*, London: Sage

Smart, C. (1984) *The Ties that Bind: Law, Marriage and the Reproduction of Patriarchal Relations*, London: Routledge and Kegan Paul

Smart, C. (1987) 'There is of course the distinction dictated by nature: Law and the Problem of Paternity', in M. Stanworth (ed.) *Reproductive Technologies*, Cambridge: Polity

Smart, C. (2005a) 'Changing Commitments: A Study of Close Kin after Divorce in England', in M. Maclean (ed.) *Family Law and Family Values*, Oxford: Hart Publishing

Smart, C. (2005b) 'Textures of Family Life: Further Thoughts on Change and Commitment', *Journal of Social Policy*, 34 (4): 541–56

Smart, C. (2006) 'Children's Narratives of Post-Divorce Family Life: From Individual Experience to an Ethical Disposition', *Sociological Review*, 54 (1): 155–70

Smart, C., and Neale, B. (1999) *Family Fragments?*, Cambridge: Polity

Smart, C., Neale, B., and Wade, A. (2001) *The Changing Experience of Childhood: Families and Divorce*, Cambridge: Polity

Smart, C., and Shipman, B. (2004) 'Visions in Monochrome: Marriage and the Individualization Thesis', *Sociology*, 55 (4): 491–509

Smith, C., and Logan, J. (2004) *After Adoption: Direct Contact and Relationships*, London: Routledge

Somerville, P. (1992) 'Homelessness and the Meaning of Home: Rooflessness and Rootlessness?', *International Journal of Urban and Regional Research*, 16 (4): 529–39

Spensky, M. (1992) 'Producers of Legitimacy: Homes for Unmarried Mothers in the 1950s', in C. Smart (ed.) *Regulating Womanhood:*

Historical Essays on Marriage, Motherhood and Sexuality, London: Routledge

Stacey, J. (1996) *In the Name of the Family*, Boston: Beacon Press

Stacey, J. (2004) 'Cruising to Familyland: Gay Hypergamy and Rainbow Kinship', *Current Sociology*, 52 (2): 181–97

Steedman, C. (1986) *Landscape for a Good Woman*, London: Virago

Steedman, C. (1992) *Past Tenses: Essays on Writing, Autobiography and History*, London: Rivers Oram Press

Sullivan, O. (2000) 'The Division of Domestic Labour: Twenty Years of Change?', *Sociology*, 34 (3): 437–56

Swartz, D. (1997) *Culture and Power: The Sociology of Pierre Bourdieu*, Chicago: University of Chicago Press

Turner, B. (1984) *The Body and Society*, Oxford: Blackwell

Turney, L. (2005) 'Paternity Secrets: Why Women Don't Tell', *Journal of Family Studies*, 11 (2): 227–48

Vogler, C. (1998) 'Money in the Household: Some Underlying Issues of Power', *Sociological Review*, 46 (4): 687–713

Vogler, C. (2005) 'Cohabiting Couples: Rethinking Money in the Household at the Beginning of the Twenty First Century', *Sociological Review*, 53 (1): 1–29

Vogler, C., Brockmann, M., and Wiggins, R. (2006) 'Intimate Relationships and Changing Patterns of Money Management at the Beginning of the Twenty First Century', *British Journal of Sociology*, 57 (3): 455–82

Wade, A. E., and Smart, C. (2002) *Facing Family Change: Children's Circumstances, Strategies and Resources*, York: York Publishing Services for the Joseph Rowntree Foundation

Warde, A. (1997) *Consumption, Food and Taste*, London: Sage

Webster, A. R. (2002) *Bitter Legacy*, Ilford, Essex: Barnardo's

Weeks, J. (1991) 'Pretended Family Relationships', in D. Clarke (ed.) *Marriage, Domestic Life and Social Change*, London: Routledge

Weeks, J., Donovan, C., and Heaphy, B. (1999) 'Everyday Experiments: Narratives of Non-Heterosexual Relationships', in E. B. Silva and C. Smart (eds) *The New Family?*, London: Sage

Weeks, J., Heaphy, B., and Donovan, C. (2001) *Same Sex Intimacies*, London: Routledge

Weston, K. (1991) *Families we Choose: Lesbian, Gays and Kinship*, New York: Columbia University Press

Williams, F. (2004) *Rethinking Families*, London: Calouste Gulbenkian Foundation

Willmott, P., and Young, M. (1973) *The Symmetrical Family*, Harmondsworth: Penguin

Wilson, E. (1977) *Women and the Welfare State*, London: Tavistock

Wright, C., and Jagger, G. (1999) 'End of Century, End of Family?: Shifting Discourses of Family Crisis', in G. Jagger and C. Wright (eds) *Changing Family Values*, London: Routledge

Young, M., and Willmott, P. (1987, orig. 1957) *Family and Kinship in East London*, Harmondsworth: Penguin

Zelizer, V. (1989) 'The Social Meaning of Money: "Special Monies" ', *American Journal of Sociology*, 95 (2): 342–77

Zelizer, V. (1994) *The Social Meaning of Money*, New York: Basic Books

Index of Names

Index of Subjects